INSIGHT POCKET GUIDE

Seattle

DISCOVERY
CHANNEL

APA PUBLICATIONS

Part of the Langenscheidt Publishing Group

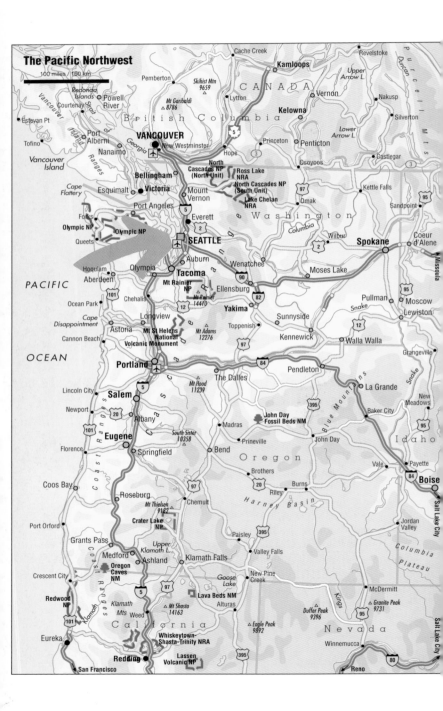

The Pacific Northwest

100 miles / 160 km

Welcome

This is one of 133 itinerary-based Pocket Guides produced by the editors of Insight Guides, whose books have set the standard for visual travel guides since 1970. With top-quality photographs and authoritative recommendations, this guidebook brings you the very best of Seattle and its surroundings in 13 itineraries devised by Insight's on-site correspondent, writer John Longenbaugh.

It begins with three full-day tours linking the essential sights: the first exploring the oldest part of Seattle and ending with its most popular attraction, the second taking in Seattle's famous marketplace and a ferry to a nearby island, and the third focusing on the intriguing neighborhood of Capitol Hill. These are followed by 10 shorter tours, exploring other interesting areas and aspects of the city, and two excursions, the first to the spectacular waterfalls in Snoqualmie, and the second to the Olympic Peninsula and the Victorian-era town of Port Townsend. Each itinerary includes ideas about where to have lunch or dine on the way. The itineraries are supported by sections on history and culture, eating out, shopping and nightlife (including recommended venues), plus a calendar of events. At the end of the guide is a practical information section covering money matters, transportation, communications, etc, and including a list of recommended hotels at all price levels.

John Longenbaugh is a freelance writer who grew up in Alaska but moved to Seattle in time to develop a passion for the arts. His years in the city have been spent writing for, among others, *Seattle Magazine*, *Seattle Weekly*, Amazon.com, Microsoft and several dot.coms that don't exist anymore. John lives on Capitol Hill, and uses his paid writing work to fund his illicit habit of playwriting. John asked that several people be thanked by name, but there are too many to list here. On his behalf, we are happy, though, to thank 'all the friends and family who kept me alive, healthy, fed and sane during my travels around Seattle.'
This edition has been updated by Giselle Smith.

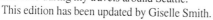

contents

EXCURSIONS

Two excursions to destinations within easy reach.

LEISURE ACTIVITIES

CALENDAR OF EVENTS

PRACTICAL INFORMATION

MAPS

CREDITS AND INDEX

Pages 2/3: houseboats on Lake Union; Seattle is surrounded by water
Pages 8/9: Seattle at night, when the Space Needle takes pride of place

History & Culture

Seattle was founded by pioneers who thought that they had discovered the Next Big Thing, and the city continues to attract people with a similar outlook. In the past 150 years or so, it has ridden out breathtaking highs and lows, without ever losing its reputation as a pleasant place to live. Newcomers may fret about the job market and a recent 'crisis of civility' in the supposedly laidback Northwest, but Seattleites of longer residence know that booms and busts are commonplace. The Emerald City (as a 1980s tourist campaign nicknamed it) has faced recession and civil unrest, and seen them to be transient. The blue waters of Puget Sound and the brooding majesty of nearby Mount Rainier are permanent, however, and anyone with the *chutzpah* to wait it out will find another boom coming along shortly.

The Duwamish and First Explorers

The Puget Sound area was a tranquil homeland long before the arrival of the Europeans. The Duwamish – the Native Americans who inhabited the area – were descended from the first people to cross over the Bering Strait more than 20,000 years ago. They were a peaceful tribe with a sophisticated society and a system of barter and trade. The region's abundant fish, game and edible plants and berries, along with a temperate climate, made the Duwamish well-fed, hospitable and creative. They rarely fought with other tribes, preferring to live peacefully in cedar-sided longhouses, and fish from ornately carved canoes.

The first European explorer of the Pacific Northwest was a British captain, George Vancouver, who landed in 1792 near what is now Everett, north of Seattle. That same year, American explorer Captain Robert Gray discovered the mouth of the Columbia River. In 1805 the Lewis & Clark Expedition reached the Pacific Coast via the Columbia, and soon afterward the British returned, establishing a fur trade. By 1824, the Hudson's Bay Company (HBC) had economic and *de facto* legal authority over those whites living in what is now British Columbia (Canada), Oregon and Washington state. However, the relentless western expansion of American settlers – as opposed to British – was pushing into Oregon by the 1830s. The HBC eventually ceded the land east of the river to the Americans, who in 1843 created the Oregon Territory.

Tumwater, the first town in what is now Washington, was founded on the southern end of Puget Sound in 1845. In 1846, the US-Canadian border was set along the 49th Parallel. Arthur and David Denny, brothers from Cherry Grove, Illinois, led a small party of family and friends along the Oregon Trail to settle

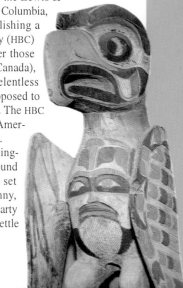

Left: 1858 Northwest scene by Alfred Jacob Miller
Right: Haida Native woodcarving

in the Willamette Valley to the south. Their aim was not farming but city building. In September of 1851 David Denny, Lee Terry and John Low went north from Portland to Alki Point. The trio started to build a cabin which Terry christened 'New York,' after his birth-place and 'Alki,' a Chinook name meaning 'by-and-by.'

When the rest of the party arrived that November, they found a discon-solate David Denny who'd caught fever, lost his provisions to skunks, and injured himself with an axe. The cabin was barely begun.

Fortune smiled in December when the brig *Leonosa* moored. With only two oxen, the Denny party harvested over 13,000ft (3,960m) of lumber and the ship took the wood to San Francisco to sell. During this first harsh winter, the native Duwamish gave and bartered food with the settlers, and were hospitable toward their new neighbors, despite the whites' nervous-ness about these 'savages.'

New York Alki proved too shallow for a port, so the following February some of the settlers set out to look for a better site. Dragging horseshoes on a line, Denny found deeper water off the eastern shore of the bay.

Doc Maynard and Chief Sealth

David Swinson Maynard, popularly known as 'Doc' Maynard, was a medical doctor, builder, blacksmith, entrepreneur and, most recently, shopkeeper in Olympia. His shop's low prices had made him exceedingly unpopular with his fellow merchants, and this moved him to explore further. Maynard set-tled at Elliott Bay, encouraged by the Denny party, who offered to move their waterfront claims and make room for his.

Maynard constructed the town's first general store, and persuaded entrepreneur Henry Yesler to locate his steam-powered sawmill at this new settlement. Yesler's mill became the center of an area known as 'Skid Road,' where a log slide sent timber skidding down the hill to the sawmill at the waterfront. The town's first boom – logging – had begun.

A genial and gregarious man, Maynard had made a friend back in Olympia, a *tyee* (chief) of the tribe living near the mouth of the nearby Duwamish River, called

Above: the Oregon Trail
Right: 'Doc' Maynard founded the first store

Chief Sealth (pronounced *see-alth* and sometimes *see-atl*). Sealth was an imposing and canny man who saw that the future of the region's indigenous population was changed forever by the arrival of the whites. Maynard, with a sense of public relations, suggested the settlers abandon the town name 'Duwamps' and adopt the anglicized 'Seattle' instead.

In 1855, Chief Sealth signed a treaty authorizing the Natives to be moved from their ancestral homes onto reservations, but the Natives weren't so keen. The 'Indian War' of 1856 started when the settlers were attacked on January 26. They fled to fortified blockhouses, and the US Navy ship *Decatur* opened fire. Two whites were killed and an undetermined number of Natives, who retreated and did not attack again.

Seattle's city fathers had been offering cash and land 'incentives' to the Northern Pacific Railroad, but in 1873 they learned that Tacoma was chosen instead as the terminus for the lucrative rail line.

By1886 much of the country was in a severe economic depression, and in the Northwest, recently arrived Chinese laborers were easy scapegoats. Many had worked on the railroads and settled, taking jobs that their white neighbors wouldn't do. Riots in Tacoma drove Chinese immigrants out of town, and unrest spread to Seattle. Mobs took to the streets, burned and looted Chinese homes and businesses, and forced over 200 Chinese onto a ship bound for San Francisco.

The Great Seattle Fire

On June 6 , 1889, a handyman named John Beck noticed a pot of glue had caught fire in a local paint store. He threw a bucket of water on the flame, which mixed with turpentine and wood shavings on the floor and caused a fiery explosion. Beck and his boss fled, and the Great Seattle Fire began. That week had been hot and dry, and central Seattle, constructed almost entirely of wood, was a tinderbox. The flames spread, the fire department was unprepared, and by nightfall virtually the entire downtown business district had burned to the ground.

Seattle had long suffered from poor planning, so this was a new opportunity, ushering in the next era of prosperity in the form of a building boom. After the fire, merchants rebuilt the city with bricks and mortar. Funds were raised from sympathetic donors across the country. Within a year, the town's population had risen from 31,000 to 37,000, largely from masons, carpenters and others coming to rebuild the city.

Originally, the town had been laid at the same level as the nearby mudflats, so plumbing backed up at high tide. During the rain, the streets became

Right: the Great Fire of 1889 destroyed much of the city

churning masses of mud, and typhoid and tuberculosis were common. The downtown area was rethought, then regraded. The ground floors were turned into basements, creating in the process the network of old storefronts later known as the Seattle 'Underground' *(see page 22).* Local boosters began projects to increase prosperity, leaving the poor and the homeless to crowd into Skid Road, which, as 'Skid Row,' became a byword for destitution.

The Gold Rush and Boeing

The next boom for Seattle was the discovery of gold in Alaska in 1897. Prospectors stampeded for the goldfields and, thanks to some canny publicity, Seattle was soon known as 'the Gateway to Alaska.' The town played merchant to over 40,000 adventurers over the next few years, and by 1900 its population had grown to 80,000.

Lumber, fish and coal were all big business in the following years. Wood in particular was important to William Boeing, a timber baron with a penchant for yachts and airplanes. He bought shipyards on the Duwamish River

and built a pontoon biplane in which he made a successful flight in 1916. Contracts from the government followed, including converting fighter planes into mail carriers. In 1927, Boeing Air Transport operated the first flight between Chicago and San Francisco. World War II was a boom for the company, thanks to the B-17 and B-29 bombers. Between the war and the present, fortunes have been mixed. There were lay-offs after the terrorist attacks of 2001, the same year Boeing moved its administrative headquarters to Chicago, but Seattle will surely weather this departure.

Above: Gold Rush miners
Left: Boeing brought an economic boom

history/culture

Lean times after World War I and increasing class-consciousness among skilled laborers led many to the cause of organized labor, in particular the International Workmen of the World, also known as the Wobblies. In 1919, the Central Labor Council held the nation's first and longest general strike, which closed Seattle down for five days. After the Wall Street crash of 1929, both labor and management faced hard times. A shantytown of the dispossessed, many from the depopulated logging camps, sprang up on the tide flats. Though destitute, the camp was well-run by its inhabitants, who started a barter economy known as 'the Republic of the Penniless.'

The Japanese attack on Pearl Harbor had a particular impact on the region. While the entry of the US into World War II was a godsend for Boeing and the nearby shipyards, it also brought into effect the Japanese Internment Act, signed by President Roosevelt, which imprisoned over 9,000 Japanese-Americans for the duration of the war. Japanese in the Seattle area were sent to camps in the neighboring states of Wyoming and Idaho, while their homes and businesses were confiscated or fell into ruin.

World's Fair to Microsoft

Seattle's economic boom after 1945 was aided by Boeing's success. In 1962 the city was host to a successful World's Fair, crowned by the Space Needle, the saucer-shaped structure that was to become Seattle's landmark. Thousands of people came to visit, and the city's presence as a leading economic player in the emerging Pacific Rim market was reaffirmed.

The turbulent and prosperous 1960s became the stagnant 1970s. As the US extricated itself from Vietnam, Boeing's military contracts dwindled. Developing the 747 passenger plane led to overspending and massive layoffs, and in 1971 a billboard went up near the city saying 'Will the last person leaving Seattle turn out the lights.' After the Vietnam War came another strand of ethnic diversity, with thousands of political refugees from Vietnam and Cambodia.

Two Bellevue natives who started their business in New Mexico in 1975 returned to their hometown in 1979, unnoticed by the local media. They were Paul Allen and Bill Gates, and their company was called Microsoft.

The 1980s began as they were to continue: with a big boom. On May 18th, 1980, the volcano called Mount St Helens erupted. The blast decimated hundreds of miles of forest and killed 57 people. Fortunately, prevailing winds sent much of the ash east, away from the city center.

Projects and profits flourished through the 1980s. Local biotech firms benefited as investors turned to technological marvels like ultrasound, gene research and, of course, personal computers. Although

Right: the World's Fair was very successful

Microsoft has been criticized and prosecuted over the years for anti-competitive business practices, its founders Bill Gates and Paul Allen have become significant public figures. Allen, who left Microsoft in 1983, became a major real-estate developer in Seattle, owner of the Seattle Seahawks football team and financier of the Experience Music Project, the futuristic rock'n'roll museum. Gates, the richest man in the world since 1999, started a charitable foundation for education, global health and population issues.

Grunge and dot.coms

The 1990s brought prosperity and artistic ferment to Seattle. Thanks to Microsoft and the many high-tech firms that sprang up around it, Puget Sound became home to many millionaires. The internet boom, led partly by Seattle-based powerhouses Amazon.com and RealNetworks, peaked in the late 1990s. Dot.com millionaires, many just in their 20s or 30s, were everywhere. Though most of the new wealth went into oversized homes and electronic gadgetry, some of the cash also made it into arts patronage. Theatres flourished. Hugely popular films were set here, as was the hit TV show *Frasier*. The music scene exploded as 'grunge.' Nirvana, Soundgarden and others were signed by major labels, and the 'Seattle Sound,' with its flannel-and-jeans image, traveled around the world.

The century ended on a dark note, however, as the annual meeting of the World Trade Organization in November of 1999 went seriously awry. A coalition of well-organized protestors clashed with ill-prepared Seattle police, and the results were a badly disrupted WTO summit, martial law and hundreds of exploding tear gas canisters. Over $10 million of damage was reported, and Seattle's reputation for 'civility' received a black eye.

Seattle Today

As the 21st century began, much of Seattle's luck turned downward. The dot.com bubble burst. Businesses announced lay-offs and cut-backs. The 2001 Mardi Gras gathering turned nasty, resulting in one death and over 70 injuries. Grunge hadn't recovered from the death of Nirvana's Kurt Cobain in 1994, and hadn't spawned a sequel.

Still, local residents draw hope from Seattle's ability to be in on whatever the Next Big Thing happens to be, and from the spirit of rebellious anti-corporate activism that the WTO protests demonstrated. This is a city that's been uneasy with success, and is making the painful transition from large town to big city. Seattle has long been livable, even profitable, but challenging times ahead may make it something that's even more valuable: profoundly interesting.

Above: Bill Gates, local boy and billionaire

HISTORY HIGHLIGHTS

pre-1851 The Duwamish, a tranquil Native American tribe, settle the region.

1851 The founding by the Denny party of 'New York Alki' ('New York by and by,') the community that later became known as Seattle.

1852 Discouraged by bad weather and poor portage, and encouraged by the charismatic 'Doc' Maynard, Denny pioneers relocate north to near today's downtown Seattle. Henry Yesler brings his steam-powered sawmill to town.

1853 The town is named in honor of 'Doc' Maynard's friend, Chief Seattle.

1855 Chief Seattle signs the Port Elliott Treaty, giving up land and establishing a reservation.

1856 Dissatisfied Natives rebel against the treaty in a one-day 'war' on January 16th, but the rebellion is efficiently and quickly quelled.

1858 Native leader Leschi is hanged for his part in the 'Treaty War.'

1861 The University of Washington is founded by Asa Mercer.

1886 Economic hard times lead to riots against Seattle's Chinese population. Stores and homes are destroyed and 200 Chinese are forced to leave.

1889 Seattle's 'Great Fire' destroys most of the downtown business area. Rebuilding immediately triggers a construction boom.

1893 The Great Northern Railway finally reaches Seattle, but so does a national recession.

1897 The Klondike Gold Rush in Alaska begins, and Seattle booms for another time.

1909 The fantastic Alaska-Yukon-Pacific Exposition is held in Seattle.

1914 The Smith Tower, Seattle's first skyscraper, is completed.

1916 Test flight of William Boeing's first plane, a pontoon biplane.

1919 The first and longest general strike in US history affects Seattle

1942 Over 9,000 Japanese-Americans are sent to nearby internment camps. Jimi Hendrix is born in the Seattle area.

1949 Sea-Tac (Seattle-Tacoma) International Airport opens.

1954 The maiden flight of the Dash-80, the prototype of Boeing's 707 passenger plane, lifts off.

1962 The Seattle World's Fair is held, crowned by the signature building, the Space Needle.

1967–1971 The 'Boeing Bust' brings bad times for the industry as demand for commercial aircraft falls.

1976 The Kingdome, a much-derided stadium for baseball and football, opens. It will be demolished in 2000 to make way for a new stadium for the Seahawks football team.

1979 Microsoft, started four years previously by locals Paul Allen and Bill Gates, moves to nearby Bellevue.

1980 Mount St Helens erupts, flattening 230 sq. miles (595 sq. km) of forest and killing 57 people.

1990–1994 The rise and fall of grunge, the Northwest rock music that finds an international audience. Kurt Cobain of Nirvana commits suicide in 1994.

1999 The city's new baseball stadium, Safeco Field, opens. Seattle hosts the World Trade Organization conference; protesters clash with police and shut the conference down on the first day.

2000 Microsoft in court: the software giant found guilty of anti-competitive business practices.

2001 Tech boom collapses, there's an earthquake and a nasty Mardi Gras riot, Boeing relocates and many jobs are under threat.

2004 The Rem Koolhaas-designed Public Library opens Downtown.

2006 The Seattle Art Museum embarks on an enormous expansion project, part of which includes the new waterfront Olympic Sculpture Park.

history/culture

Seattle

City Itineraries

1. PIONEER SQUARE TO THE SPACE NEEDLE *(see maps, p18–19 and p38)*

From the birthplace of Seattle in Pioneer Square, via a quirky and informative tour of Seattle's 'Underground' to Pike Place Market for lunch, then a Monorail trip to Experience Music Project and the Space Needle. The tour finishes with dinner and drinks in Belltown.

Starting point is Pioneer Square, an easy walk for visitors staying in the city; otherwise most public transportation connects to the center.

The hometown of what is now an international 'coffee culture,' Seattleites don't go in for breakfast in a big way, preferring a latte in a 'go-cup' with, at most, a muffin. But since our tour begins in historic Pioneer Square, surrounded by some of the classiest architecture in Seattle (Victorian-Romanesque, to be precise), we begin our day at **Zeitgeist Art and Coffee** (tel: 206 583-0497; 171 S. Jackson; zeitgeistcoffee.com).

Like many locally owned coffee shops, this cafe/gallery offers free wireless internet access (known as Wi-Fi) to its many laptop-carrying customers. Another Pioneer Square coffee shop where the customers stick around is the **Elliott Bay Bookstore Café** (tel: 206 682-6664; 101 S Main; www.elliottbaybook.com). Here, you'll also see some laptops (free wireless), but more likely the patrons will be reading books purchased upstairs at the Elliott Bay Book Company (tel: 206 624-6600). This local institution has a devoted following of folks who come for the excellent selection of used and new books, and the almost-nightly author readings and book signings.

Pioneer Square

Now, off to the Seattle Underground Tour. Skirting **Occidental Park**, head north up 1st Avenue toward the big totem pole in **Pioneer Square**, the small cobblestoned area between Cherry and James. Here is a **bust of Chief Seattle**, Seattle's namesake, with words from his famous speech, as well as the **totem pole** from the Tlingit Indians of Southeast Alaska. This is the second such pole in this spot. The first came from what was thought to be an abandoned Native village and was accidentally burned. When the city fathers sent a check to the Natives to carve another, a note came back with thanks for payment of the first – stolen – pole, and offering a second pole for another payment. The check was sent and the result still stands. Nearby is a **glass-and-iron pergola**, built in 1909. The structure was destroyed by a truck in 2001, but after nearly $4 million was spent on restoration, it stands elegantly on its former site.

Left: downtown Seattle overlooks Elliott Bay
Right: bust of Chief Seattle in Pioneer Square

Go Underground

The **Underground Tour** runs year round (seasonal changes to times; call 206 682-4646 for schedule and info; 608 1st Avenue; www.undergroundtour.com; admission fee). Bill Spiedel, a newspaperman, started a guided tour of the basements, passageways and underground streets created after the Great Fire *(see page 14)*, to help raise funds for the preservation of Pioneer Square.

Bill was more fascinated by the town's history of booze-halls, brothels and brawls, many of which were in the square, than in the 'official' accounts of the pioneers. The original underground tours were led by flashlight and through puddles of water, but while their current incarnation is well-lit and dry, Spiedel's high spirits are still plenty in evidence.

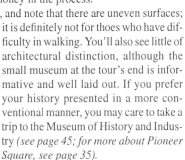

While the guides never let history stand in the way of a good joke, the tour is an excellent overview of Seattle's origins and early days, and a timely reminder that Seattle's founding fathers – like the current city leaders – had a singular obsession with furthering their careers and making money in the process.

The tour takes about 90 minutes, and note that there are uneven surfaces;

it is definitely not for thoes who have difficulty in walking. You'll also see little of architectural distinction, although the small museum at the tour's end is informative and well laid out. If you prefer your history presented in a more conventional manner, you may care to take a trip to the Museum of History and Industry *(see page 45; for more about Pioneer Square, see page 35).*

Turn right from Pioneer Square and walk up 1st Avenue toward downtown Seattle. This area, once run-down and seedy, has been massively redeveloped and is now all condominiums, upscale boutiques and restaurants. There are reminders of its shady past, however, like an adult video store and the peepshow 'The Lusty Lady,' whose marquee is often charmingly witty.

Above: the entrance to Pike Place Market. **Above Right:** totem pole in Pioneer Square
Right: Seattle Center fountain is fun for kids

Eight blocks up is the **Seattle Art Museum** (1st and University; Tues–Sun 10am–5pm, Thur to 9pm; tel: 206 654-3100; www.seattleartmuseum.org; admission fee), hard to miss with its distinctive 48-ft (15-m) high signature sculpture, Jonathan Borofsky's *The Hammering Man*. If you've got time, SAM features distinguished traveling shows, plus permanent exhibits from other eras and cultures, including Interior House posts from a Native village in British Columbia, a Jackson Pollock and a masterpiece by Van Dyck. Two more blocks up 1st to Pike Street and we've reached the soul of Seattle's cultural and mercantile life, the **Pike Place Market**. Opened in 1907, this is the longest continually operated public market in the United States. Preservation efforts, local crafts and produce and an absence of large franchise outlets contribute to the market's enduring popularity with locals and visitors alike.

Now would be a good time for lunch. Vendors offer humbows, sandwiches, salads and wonderful, fresh seafood. There are also some excellent restaurants and cafés right in the market, including Bolivian cuisine at Copacabana (tel: 206 622-6359) with spicy shrimp soup and outstanding paella; French cuisine at Maximilien (tel: 206 682-7270, and homey cafeteria food at Lowell's (tel: 206 622-2036), most of which offer great views of Elliott Bay. You'll be having breakfast in the market tomorrow *(see page 26)*, so there's no need to look around now.

Monorail to the Seattle Center

After lunch, leave the market where you entered, at 1st and Pike, and turn away from the harbor toward the city along Pike. Turn left on 4th Avenue and walk one block to Pine (don't worry if you get confused between Pike and Pine, everyone in town does). You're now in Westlake Park facing the upscale **Westlake Center**, a shopping mall located between two bastions of Northwest retail therapy, **Bon Marché** (left) and **Nordstrom** (right). Nordstrom department store, a family business, was born right here in the city, and now has branches across America. Cross the street into the center. Shopping here includes classy chain boutiques and a food court. Then board the **Monorail** for the 2-minute trip to the **Seattle Center** (small fee). That's the only stop. A local joke is tourists asking for a map so they don't get

lost. The ride, whizzing over the top of the city, is fast and fun.

Seattle Center has a small amusement park, but the main attractions here are the Experience Music Project (EMP), the Pacific Science Center, the Space Needle and a Children's Museum, as well as three of Seattle's main stage theatres; Intiman, the Seattle Children's Theatre and the Seattle Repertory *(see map on page 38)*. Free and delightful is the Seattle Center's fountain, a silver dome with jets of water choreographed to music. Children dash through the water on hot days, shrieking with glee.

Guitar Heaven

The **Experience Music Project** (EMP) (open daily 9am–11pm summer months; until 5pm Mon–Thur, 6pm Fri–Sat fall, winter and spring; telephone: 206 367-5483 or 206 EMPLIVE; www.emplive.com; admission fee) is Seattle Center's newest attraction, and already one of its most popular. What billionaire Paul Allen requested from the architect, Frank Gehry, was 'swoopiness,' and the controversial design has plenty of it. The vast concrete-and-metal structure was inspired by shapes of rock guitars that Gehry supposedly cut apart for inspiration. From a distance, its blobbish form in scarlet, magenta and silver seems about to ambush the base of the unsuspecting Space Needle, and the Monorail actually travels through it on the way to the Center Station.

The ticket price to EMP is steep, but you get a lot in high-tech equipage, including a hand-held wand wired to a small computer and a pair of headphones. As you pass through the museum, you can download information from the exhibits to hear additional music and narration, and 'bookmark' exhibits for later scrutiny. The museum has sections on blues, jazz, early and progressive rock'n'roll, exhibits on '60s icons Jimi Hendrix (born in Seattle), Eric Clap-

ton, Janis Joplin and Bob Dylan, and a gallery devoted to the birth and development of the 'Northwest sound' that spawned grunge. Other attractions include a hands-on gallery where patrons can mix music, take computer-led guitar lessons and participate in an electronic drum circle; a 'motion platform' exhibit called 'The Artist's Journey' and the vast 'Sky Church,' where the world's largest video display serves as the backdrop for live acts.

Nearby, the **Pacific Science Center** (daily 10am–5pm, weekends until 6pm; tel: 206 443-2001; www.pacsci.org; admission fee), a longtime favorite, features many levels of interactive exhibits that children and inquisitive

adults will enjoy, like a chance to examine levers and counterweights, explore dinosaurs and robots, and even watch up close the tunnelings of naked mole rats. An **IMAX cinema** and a **planetarium** can be visited for an additional price.

You can gawp at the foot of the **Space Needle** (Sun–Thur 9am–11pm, Fri–Sat 9am–midnight; tel: 206 443 2111; admission fee) or take the trip up to the top *(see page 38)*. In either case, after a long afternoon at Seattle Center, it's time to find some food. Unless you adore food courts (there's another one here, at Center House, where the Monorail pulls in), let's head back Downtown again.

Belltown

Have dinner and maybe drinks afterward in **Belltown**, the neighborhood that borders Downtown to the north of Pike Place Market. To get there, leave Westlake and walk down Pine to 1st Avenue. Turn right and walk into Belltown. Here are four distinctive restaurants to choose from, depending on your mood. If you're up for a splurge, head for El Gaucho (2505 1st Avenue, tel: 206 728-1337; www.elgaucho.com), a swank, retro steakhouse that's the place to see and be seen. For some of the city's best upscale seafood, head to Flying Fish (2234 1st Avenue, tel: 206 728-8595; www.flyingfish-seattle.com), where everything is fresh and artfully presented.

The Queen City Grill (2201 1st Avenue, tel: 206 443-0975; www.queencitygrill.com), open since 1987, is a high-end establishment serving 'seafood and chops,' including white gulf prawns, Dungeness crab cakes and Flat Iron steak. This is a place to settle in for the evening, as the wait staff are friendly and professional, the drinks are excellent and the place draws a large number of Belltown's beautiful people from midnight onwards. Finally, for anyone on a budget, head up to the Frontier Room (2203 1st Avenue, tel: 206 956-RIBS; www.frontierroom.com), where the specialties are beef brisket and ribs, with a Western motif.

Left: two views of the Frank Gehry-designed Experience Music Project
Above: Pacific Science Center in Seattle Center

2. PIKE PLACE MARKET AND ACROSS ELLIOTT BAY (see map, p18–19)

Breakfast at Pike Place Market, then explore the attractions on the waterfront. Jump onto a Washington State Ferry for a trip to a neighboring island, then be back in Seattle in time for dinner.

Start from Pike Place Market.

We return on our second day to the **Pike Place Market**. You'll find that an early morning visit varies significantly from a visit in the middle of the day. If you're very early, you'll see the arrival of flowers, produce

and fish, brought by trucks from the Puget Sound area and beyond. Local coffee shops, including the original Starbucks (founded here in 1971), open bright and early as well. For an early morning treat, try coffee and a pastry from La Panier Very French Bakery (tel: 206 441-3669; www.lepanier.com), or a huge sticky roll from The Cinnamon Works (tel: 206 583-0085).

Coffee and pastry in hand, enter the market and descend the stairs to the lower level. From here you join the Hillclimb steps, which take you all the way down to Western Avenue. An elevator service is also available. Cross Western under the Alaskan Way viaduct and you'll come to the **Waterfront Streetcar**. This popular line runs all the way from the International District along the full length of the Seattle waterfront with convenient stops along the way. Note: the streetcar will be off the tracks during construction of the Seattle Art Museum's Olympic Sculpture Park, but is expected to be in service again by summer 2007.

In either case, cross over to Alaskan Way and the waterfront near Pier 62. Immediately to your right is the **Seattle Aquarium** (daily 10am–5pm, until 7pm in summer; tel: 206 386-4320; www.seattleaquarium.org; admission fee). This first-rate center exhibits fish and other marine life native to Puget Sound, and has working models of reefs, tidepools and ocean floors. The fish ladder, exotic creatures like the lion fish and the eels (electric and otherwise) attract a lot of attention, but it's the lively seals and otters that capture the ever-attentive crowd.

Coming up are Piers 55 and 56, where a number of private cruise lines offer trips around the bay, up and through the interesting Ballard Locks and out to **Tillicum Village** on Blake Island, a nearby Native American attraction that presents a blend of regional traditions. Continue to your left, towards **Pier 54** (tel: 206 624-6852), enjoying the sea breeze and the boats on Elliott Bay, till you reach **Ye Olde Curiosity Shop** (1001 Alaskan Way; tel: 206 682-5844; www.yeoldecuriosityshop.com). You may see this warehouse-like store as a vast tourist trap, and in one sense you'd be right. Filled with key

Above: a chili day at Pike Place Market
Above right: Ivar's Acres of Clams is famous. **Right:** ferry across Elliott Bay

chains, license plates and assorted other gewgaws, the shop has been huckstering to visitors since 1899. Some of the more unusual items are in the back: mummies, shrunken heads, and grains of rice engraved with texts or portraits of sports celebrities; the place also has an aroma unlike anything else on earth. This is the store in which to buy Mexican Jumping Beans, assuming this is how you'd like to remember Seattle.

Next door to the shop is **Ivar's Acres of Clams**, a venerable seafood restaurant founded by local singer, raconteur and personality Ivar Haglund. Seagull feeding is encouraged from the side deck of the restaurant, as evidenced by a charming statue of Ivar on the waterfront, feeding a quartet of birds. Haglund's long career in town included the founding of the town's first aquarium, and many locals still remember him wheeling one of his seals about town in a perambulator.

A Ferry Ride Across the Bay

Now we come to Pier 51, the **Washington State Ferries** terminal. Since you've made it to the ferry dock, you get to choose how to spend your afternoon: do you want a trip across the water to Bainbridge Island, or to Bremerton? **Bainbridge Island,** which in 2005 was named the No. 2 community to live in by *Money Magazine*, is a 35-minute ferry ride, and ferries leave roughly every hour. Close proximity to Seattle means that many of the island's 22,000 residents commute to work across the water. It wasn't always a bedroom community, however. **Port Blakely**, to the south of Winslow, was for a time home to the world's largest sawmill, and the **Hall Brothers' Shipyard** was a flourishing business. There were also small farms and berry-

growers, many owned by Japanese-Americans whose internment during World War II was disastrous for the island's economy and the community's well-being. Now **Winslow**, the island's major town, is an appealing place which serves as the main shopping center for Bainbridge's residents.

From the ferry landing, follow the blue salmon on the sidewalk to your left for the block and a half into downtown Winslow and Winslow Way, the town's main street. If you'd like a short wilderness fix, take a sharp left turn before entering town, where there is a brief, pleasant nature trail that winds around and back to town.

In Winslow itself are the usual craft stores, boutiques and antique shops of a typical tourist town, as well as a few cafés that are favorites of island residents: Bainbridge Bakers (140 Winslow Way, tel: 206 842-1822); Blackbird Bakery (210 Winslow Way E, tel: 206 780-1322), and Pegasus Coffee House (131 Parfitt Way SW, tel: 206 842-6725), offering locally roasted coffee daily and live music on weekends. Café Nola (101 Winslow Way E, tel: 206 842-3822, www.cafenola.com) is a European-style bistro serving brunch on weekends, lunch on weekdays and dinner every night.

Rent a Boat

You can leave Winslow Way and head down Madison Street toward the Harbor Side Marina. Here, dozens of private craft berth at the site where Seattle's 'Mosquito Fleet' once served. This was the scrappy collection of small private vessels that stood in for a ferry service among the various island communities from the 1860s through the 1940s, until the establishment of

the Washington State Ferry Service. A boardwalk runs along the marina, all the way up to the **Harbour Public House**. From the porch is a fine view of the water and the Seattle skyline. If you'd like to get out onto the water, you can rent kayaks, canoes or a swan boat at Back of Beyond (tel: 206 842-9229), at the dock by Waterfront Park.

If you've brought over either a bike or a car (you can rent a bike at the B.I.Cycle Shop at 162 Bjune Drive SE, tel: 206 842-6412; www.b-i-cycle.com), you might head out of Winslow a little ways for some trail hiking. Alternatively, visit the tran-

Above: Bainbridge Island from the ferry
Left: Bainbridge Island Winery

quil **Bloedel Reserve** (7571 Dolphin Drive NE, tel: 206 842-7631 for reservations; www.bloedelreserve.org; admission fee), a limited-visitor park that features a series of contemplative gardens, or the **Bainbridge Gardens** (9415 Miller Road NE), whose owner Junkoh Harui continues the business begun by his father. Another stop that's easy to make – if you've got wheels – is the **Bainbridge Island Vineyards and Winery** (8989 Day Road E, tel: 206 842-9463) a few miles outside town and which is open for tastings Friday through Sunday.

Bremerton

While **Bremerton** also has a small downtown area with occasional shops for tourists, it's a very different community from Bainbridge. Since 1891 the US Navy has been central to this town's economy, first with a station and then with Naval Shipyards. The town prospered on these services until the 1970s, when businesses migrated to other places. Work at the shipyards now remains steady, but there have been recent attempts to transform the community's blue-collar ambience into something more hospitable to visitors, and it's this unfinished, almost overly-welcoming atmosphere that makes it an intriguing place to spend the afternoon.

There are two ferries to Bremerton, a car ferry and a slightly faster passenger-only ferry, but both trips take about an hour. The trip is glorious, sliding out of Elliott Bay into **Sinclair Inlet**, past dozens of beautiful coastal homes and a couple of small communities.

Bremerton has three downtown museums and several art galleries. The **Naval Memorial Museum of the Pacific** (tel: 360 479-7447) is located a

few blocks north of the ferry terminal at 402 Pacific Avenue. Admission to this small but packed museum is free, and the exhibits include models of famous naval vessels, as well as a history of the base using artifacts, photos and dioramas. Anchored nearby on the renovated waterfront park is the **USS** *Turner Joy* (daily May–Sept, otherwise Fri–Sun; 300 Washington Beach Avenue, tel: 360 792-2457; go to www.ussturnerjoy.org; admission fee), infamous for her involvement in the Gulf of Tonkin incident, which decisively drew the United States into the Vietnam War. The tourist center near the ship also offers a seasonal tour of several decommissioned vessels which are currently berthed near the shipyards.

Up on 4th Street is the very friendly **Kitsap County Historical Society Museum** (tel: 360 479-6226; www.waynes.net/kchsm; admission fee), a slightly sparse center of information on the history of the region. Like Bremerton itself, the museum's focus on industry and blue-collar occupations is an interesting contrast to the high-tech professional lifestyles across the water in Seattle.

Right: sculpture on Bremerton boardwalk

The renaissance Bremerton has been experiencing in recent years has brought a new conference center and a downtown waterfront hotel, as well as a handful of galleries (many showing local artists) and quaint shops. Downtown also has pleasant stops for just hanging out. Coffee Oasis (822 Burwell Street; tel: 360 373-0461) is a cozy café with a friendly atmosphere and a nice selection of pastries, while Cornerstone Coffee (435 Pacific Avenue, tel: 360 479-3334; www.cornerstonecoffeeshop.com) offers live music, free wireless internet access and stays open late whenever there's a show at the **Admiral Theatre** next door. At both locations you're likely to find yourself pleasantly engaged in conversation with the locals, who are involved in earnest efforts to make their community accessible to visitors.

Back to Seattle, and dinner in the marketplace. Come evening, the vendors and many cafés have closed, but some fine restaurants remain open. Particularly recommended is Il Bistro (93A Pike Street, tel: 206 682-3049; www.ilbistro.net), located in the cobbled alley just to the left of *Rachel the*

Pig, the market's icon. Il Bistro is a traditional Italian restaurant with a superb wine list and gnocchi that shouldn't be missed, though you might well be tempted by the 'penne con melanzane' with grilled eggplant. The atmosphere is dark and jazzy, perfect for an intimate evening. For something livelier, The Pink Door (1919 Post Alley, tel: 206 443-3241; www.thepinkdoor.net) is another Italian restaurant, this one slightly boisterous with ongoing cabaret and musical acts in the bar. Their seafood pasta is particularly good.

Finally, if you're on the ball with reservations you might squeeze into Matt's in the Market (94 Pike Street, No. 32, tel: 206 467-7909). Popular for lunch as well as dinner, this tiny

Above: bar in Bremerton
Left: *Rachel the Pig*, Pike Place Market icon

third-floor restaurant offers entirely fresh seafood along with market vegetables, served with innovative sauces. When we say 'tiny,' we mean it; your server can be counted to know the menu, because chances are, she'll take your order, then head back to the grill to cook it.

3. A DAY IN CAPITOL HILL (SEE MAP, P18–19)

Capitol Hill is Seattle's most varied neighborhood, with distinguished houses, a beautiful city park and good nightlife. Wear comfortable shoes as we'll be strolling up some steep hills.

Begin at Bellevue and Olive Way, just a few blocks past the overpass that divides Capitol Hill from Downtown. Get there by a 43 bus, which stops about a half block away.

Capitol Hill, on a slope above Downtown, has gradually evolved from a quiet residential area into a varied collection of shops, clubs, coffeehouses and restaurants. Since the 1970s, it's been the central home for Seattle's gay community, as well as a popular hang-out for youth culture, a hotbed of alternative or 'fringe' theatres, and a major center for independent bookstores and fashionable boutiques.

Coffee, Coffee Everywhere

Cross the street and walk up Olive Way. This morning begins at some fine coffee shops with different atmospheres, as befits this eclectic neighborhood; visit whichever appeals to you. Up the hill, past antique shops and specialist record stores, and across the street (watch for speeding traffic on the corner of Denny; this is a bad place for turns) is Coffee Messiah (1554 E. Olive Way, tel: 206 861-8233; www.coffeemessiah.com), filled with local art, iconoclastic imagery, good coffee and customers with a sense of humor.

Continue up Olive and bypass, please, the large Starbucks on your right. For all the Seattle 'lifestyle-friendly' corporations – from Microsoft and Amazon to Starbucks and Nordstrom – the city is known for, there is also a fiercely defended anti-corporate spirit. And Capitol Hill has plenty of other coffee shops to visit instead.

Up a block or so at Belmont is B&O Espresso (204 Belmont E, tel: 206 322-5028), a full café with a wide selection of pastries and such caffeinated delicacies as a white chocolate mocha. They do a great light menu called 'twisted tapas' as well, and there is a full bar. Although it's a bit early for a drink, remember the location of The Stumbling Monk across the street (1635 E Olive

Right: Capitol Hill's Coffee Messiah coffeehouse: you either love it or hate it

Way, tel: 206 860-0916). It's a small pub and beer shop specializing in Belgian-brewed beers and Northwest wines.

Continue up Olive Way for about another block and a half and you'll come to the Online Coffee Company (1720 E Olive Way, tel: 206 328-3731), one of Seattle's more comfortable on-line cafés, with plush leather couches and 30 minutes' free internet time with the cost of a beverage.

Regards to Broadway

Continue to Broadway, and turn right. If you still haven't had your caffeine fix, head down a block and take a left on Denny. Here you'll find the favorite coffee shop of many Seattleites: Espresso Vivace Roasteria (901 E. Denny Way, tel: 206 860-5869; www.espressovivace.com). If you'd rather not take the time to go inside, Vivace has an enormously popular sidewalk bar two blocks farther north on Broadway at Thomas Street. The metal chairs and tables on the sidewalk next to the walk-up counter are filled with patrons almost any time of day or night (both Vivaces open from 6:30am–11pm daily).

For the next four blocks, you're in the center of Capitol Hill's main shopping area, with restaurants, boutiques and a wide variety of stores and ser-

vices. Here is some of the city's best people-watching, as young pierced skater punks jostle with suits, Goths brush by gay couples, all in a tolerant and generally pleasant atmosphere scarcely marred by the young street kids begging for spare change. (A note to the tender-hearted: before you hand over some cash, check the quality of their clothing. While there are hard cases in the neighborhood, panhandling is also an afternoon's diversion for some middle-class kids.)

Keep a pleasant pace along Broadway. At Harvard, Broadway takes a slight turn to the left. Cross over, and follow the residential street it becomes, which is filled with older houses and the occasional new building or apartment house. Three blocks along you'll come to E Prospect. Turn right and cross the road at 10th, then continue on up the same street.

Within two blocks you can turn left into **Volunteer Park**, or continue alongside the Park to 14th and Prospect. On your trip you'll see lovely older houses to your right, reminders of the time when this neighborhood was known as 'Millionaires' Row.' On 14th (or through the Park, your choice), turn left as you face the **Volunteer Park Water Tower**.

Volunteer Park is in many ways the crown jewel of the efforts begun in 1903 by the Olmsted Brothers, sons of the visionary architect of New York's

Above: the water tower in Capitol Hill's Volunteer Park
Above Right: Seattle Asian Art Museum. **Right:** Capitol Hill-billies

Central Park. Hired by the city to develop a series of parks, they devised green spaces winding through Seattle in two wide loops and linked by landscaped parkways. Volunteer Park, which had been a city graveyard, was transformed into 45 acres (18 hectares) of winding paths, pleasant groves and scenic vistas.

The Water Tower's 95-ft (29-m) summit offers a fine view over the city, as well as an informative exhibit on the Olmsteds. Its 106 steps are even and relatively easy for most people to climb. After the tower, either take a left or a right and continue into the park.

On your right, between two stone camels, is the **Seattle Asian Art Museum** (daily 10am–5pm, Thur to 9pm, closed Mon; tel: 206 654-3100; www.seattleartmuseum.org; admission fee), housed in an elegant 1931 Art Deco building. This was the Seattle Art Museum up till 1991, when that museum moved Downtown. The original founders, Richard Fuller and his mother, Margaret E. MacTavish Fuller, were enthusiasts of Asian art and artifacts, and their collection became the central component of this museum. From the front steps of SAAM is one of the best-orchestrated views in Seattle, the Space Needle framed by sculptor Isamu Noguchi's *Black Sun*, known locally as 'the large black donut.'

Take a right out of SAAM and follow the main path. Just ahead you'll come to a handsome statue of William Seward, the US Secretary who in 1867 organized the buying of Alaska from Russia for the excellent price of 2¢ an acre.

Behind the statue is the **Volunteer Park Conservatory** (free), a small gem of a greenhouse patterned after London's Crystal Palace and shipped from New York to Seattle in 1912. The five galleries of the collection feature over 800 plants, including cacti and prize-winning orchids.

Now you can either return to the tower or take a detour to **Lake View Cemetery**. Leaving the conservatory, turn left and follow the road as it curves down toward 15th Avenue. Turn left and walk along for about a block to E Garfield. The entrance to Lake View Cemetery is on your left (it's open until dusk; free).

Graves of the Famous

Here are the graves of 'Doc' Maynard and his wife, the Dennys, the Mercers, and Chief Sealth's daughter, Princess Angeline. On a circle road some way into the graveyard, on the east side just below the roadway, are the simple black headstones of martial artist and movie star Bruce Lee and his son Brandon, who both died tragically as young men, the elder Lee in 1973 and his son, also an actor, 20 years later. They were Seattle residents for only a short time, but chose to be buried here.

Walking back to 15th, turn right and start along the pleasant tree-filled residential street. After five blocks is the main mercantile center of 15th, a more sedate version of Broadway, which is several blocks below.

If you're ready for a late lunch, here are a few recommendations along this street. On your right and across the road is the Coastal Kitchen (429 15th Avenue E, telephone: 206 322-1145; www.chowfoods.com/coastal), a moderately-priced restaurant with a changing menu (strong on seafood) featuring a different coastal region's cuisine every three months.

A little farther down the block, on the other side of the street, you'll find the Bagel Deli (340 15th Avenue E, tel: 206 322-2471), where the kosher bagels are boiled and baked onsite. Cross the street again and head south another block and you'll find comfortable couches and good coffee, sandwiches and service amid local artwork at Victrola Coffee and Art (411 15th Avenue E, tel: 206 325-6520).

Above: Volunteer Park's 1912 conservatory
Right: martial artist Bruce Lee and son: RIP

After a bite and a libation, perhaps it's time for some shopping. Particularly recommended is Take 2 at 430 15th Avenue, tel: 206 324-2459, known for excellent quality contemporary consignment clothes, and there are many more stores where this comes from *(see 'Shopping' on page 68)*. Continue down 15th to E John Street, where there's a view to admire of Puget Sound and the Space Needle.

Turn right and walk down to Broadway. On your left is the Capitol Hill branch of Twice Sold Tales (905 E John, tel: 206 324-2421; www.twicetold.com), which offers crowded shelves of used books, and lots of cats.

You're now back at the corner of Broadway and John, the center of Capitol Hill's social activity. From here you can return to Downtown via a 43 bus, or consider more strolling toward your left, in the direction of the Pike/Pine corridor, for more shopping and interesting restaurants and clubs.

4. PIONEER SQUARE, SAFECO FIELD AND THE INTERNATIONAL DISTRICT *(see map, p18–19)*

A return visit to Pioneer Square, Seattle's original neighborhood, a trip to the state-of-the-art sports stadium and then a stroll through the International District, ending up in a peaceful park. Walking is best in this traffic-congested area.

Start at 2nd and Yesler, at Smith Tower.

We start our tour at 2nd and Yesler, not far from **Pioneer Square**. Our first destination is **Smith Tower** (506 Second Avenue, tel: 206 622-4004; www.smith-tower.com), which was Seattle's most recognizable landmark before the raising of the Space Needle in 1962. To many locals it's still a favorite, a magnificently antiquated skyscraper that is said to have been the tallest building west of the Mississippi when it was built in 1914. It still has a glorious gilt lobby, and the elevators have human operators. For a small fee you can make a trip up to the observation deck on the 35th floor, but check the online calendar before you visit as the tower is a popular venue and is often closed due to a private event being held inside.

Leaving the tower, turn left and walk down the 2nd Avenue S Extension for about a block. Then turn slightly left (a hard left would take you down S Washington) and walk down 2nd Avenue S. After a block, you'll find one of the most charming parks in the city, the miniature **Waterfall Garden**, on the corner of 2nd Avenue S and S Main. Built, believe it or not, to honor the birthplace of United Parcel Service, it's a popular place for lunchtime readers and quiet contemplation.

From Waterfall Garden, take a right and continue down S Main Street about a block. You'll find yourself at the pedestrian section of Occidental Street. To your left and right are art galleries lining both sides of the street. This is the center of a lot of activity during the Art Walk, held the first Thursday of every month, when all of Pioneer Square's various galleries hold open house and invite patrons in for cheese, wine and schmoozing.

Seahawks and Mariners

After browsing, take a left and cross the street. You're now headed down Occidental S toward the two sports stadia. The Kingdome was imploded in 2000 to clear space for the Seahawks' new football stadium. The pyrotechnics were cheered at the time, but in the tightening economy, a lot of folks were left wondering if it was such a good idea, particularly as the Kingdome – ugly but solid enough to last another hundred years – had not even been paid off.

Qwest Field, which opened in 2002 and got its corporate-sponsor name in 2004, is open for guided tours every day events are not scheduled. Telephone 206 381 7582 (admission fee) for availability, and be sure to wear comfortable shoes.

Qwest is an appropriate match for state-of-the-art **Safeco Field**, the home of Seattle's baseball team, the Mariners. Safeco is one of the most expensive sports stadiums in the world, and the money is abundantly on display. It's impressive from the outside, but sports enthusiasts will want to join a guided tour (tel: 206 346-4001; admission fee) which departs from the sports store adjacent to the stadium two or three times a day, depending on season and baseball schedules. The stadium, which holds 47,000 people, has a huge retractable roof (using enough steel for a 50-story skyscraper), and the field is real grass, a blend of Kentucky blue grass and rye grass.

After gaping at this temple to professional sports, turn left up S Royal Brougham, between the two stadia, and walk down 4th Avenue S until you come to S Dearborn Street, where you turn right. Walk down S Dearborn for two blocks, then turn left.

Truly International

Uwajimaya Village (600 5th Avenue S, tel: 206 624-6248; www.uwaji-maya.com) is this part of the city's most popular destination, a gigantic Asian supermarket with aisles of Asian food, both fresh and prepared, delicacies, kitchen accessories, furnishings and products rarely seen in the West. For almost five decades the store has been a cornerstone of Seattle's International District, first as a small retail store and fish-cake manufacturing company, then in the 1960s as a low-key supermarket, and finally transforming in 2000 into its current, exciting, form. The crayon-bright colors of the foods and packaging make it fun even for non-shoppers.

The **International District** is an eclectic mixture of Asian peoples, including Chinese, Japanese, Laotian, Korean and Taiwanese. Twice in Seattle's history its population was decimated by racism – the Chinatown riots of 1886 and again with the internment of Japanese-Americans in 1942 in response to the bombing of Pearl Harbor in World War II – but these days it's a bustling, agreeably shabby neighborhood that is being scrutinized by beady-eyed developers.

There are many good opportunities for shopping, supping and sightseeing in the International District. Although it's a relatively small neighborhood, the stores, small businesses and restaurants are authentic and busy. Think about a trip up the road to **Viet Wah** (1032 S Jackson Street, tel: 206 328-3557), an Asian supermarket significantly less expensive and less sanitized than Uwajimaya, around which excellent Vietnamese restaurants are clustered.

When you're ready to join the tour again, make your way to Seventh and S Jackson Street, and the **Wing Luke Asian Museum** (407 7th Avenue S, tel: 206 623-5124; www.wingluke.org; small admission fee, free on Thur). Named for Seattle's first Chinese-American city council member, this museum celebrates the diversity of ten major ethnic heritages, as well as the unique community that has developed in the International District. In 1995, the Wing Luke received an award of excellence from President Clinton. (Note: the museum is currently conducting a capital campaign and hopes to move into new – and better – permanent premises not far away in 2007.)

Exit the museum and turn left. Take another left on S Jackson Street and walk down one block to Maynard Street, then take a right to cross the street. Now walk up Maynard in front of you for two blocks, and you'll come to **Kobe Terrace Park**. This charming and tranquil area contains a series of small gardens lovingly tended by locals, in addition to a colossal stone lantern donated by Seattle's Japanese sister city, Kobe. There is a fine panoramic view of the city from the park.

city itineraries

5. THE SPACE NEEDLE *(see map below)*

Take a trip up Seattle's most famous landmark.

The Space Needle is located at Seattle Center, and is accessible by car, foot, bus or via the Monorail.

Seattle's number one tourist attraction, the **Space Needle** (Sun–Thur 9am–11pm, Fri–Sat 9am–midnight; tel: 206 443 2111; admission fee), is a 1960s fantasy of what the 21st century might look like. Now that we're actually *in* the 21st century, it looks gracefully quaint. The idea of a 'saucer on a stick' was sketched on a napkin by Eddie Carlson in 1959, the man who was president of the upcoming Seattle World's Fair. Carlson's idea was turned to reality by architect John Graham, who came up with the elegant tripod form that towers 605ft (184m) above the nearby buildings.

The theme of the 1962 fair was the 21st century, with visionary exhibits that included a 'Spacearium,' and a 'World of Tomorrow.' It also highlighted that other still-in-use relic, the Monorail. While visitors loved the Needle, there was agreement that its colors, 'Re-entry Red,' 'Astronaut Gold' and 'Orbital Green,' could use a change. Its current hue is custom-made for the structure – 'Space Needle White.'

Above: 1962 vision of the 21st century

Despite its slender base, the Needle is a remarkably secure building. A structural engineer happened to be at the site during the 2001 earthquake that measured 6.8 on the Richter Scale, and after his inspections the Needle was open for business that same day. This is because the base, sunk 30ft (9m) into the ground, weighs almost as much as the visible structure, so the center of gravity is just above the ground. Recent renovations have focused on its base, which has been replaced with a graceful two-story spiral entryway that curves around a central dome housing the gift shop, the aptly named **SpaceBase**. The trinkets in SpaceBase are of a higher caliber than before, with a retro section, an 'executive toy' section and a 'Seattle section,' featuring the work of local artists.

SkyGuide

Visitors stand in line to board one of the gleaming, chrome elevators. With a SkyGuide at the helm, it and you then whoosh up a speedy 520ft (158.5m) to the top. With the gift shop now downstairs, the indoor **Observation Deck** is spacious and uncluttered, perfect for gazing at that drop-dead gorgeous, 360° view of Puget Sound, Lake Washington, Lake Union, Mount Rainier, and the Cascade and Olympic mountain ranges. If you decide to visit at night, the city huddled down below turns into a wonderful black blanket interspersed with twinkling lights. Day or night, be sure to check out the view using one of the (free) telescopes. The **SkyCafe** has snacks, while six interactive game stations – designed by Seattle-based Gamemaker – includes facts and trivia. Walk around the perimeters by yourself, or join one of the SkyGuide-led tours.

Locals have long said that the food in the Needle's restaurant is mediocre, but that's not really true anymore. Renamed **SkyCity** (tel: 206 905-2100; www.spaceneedle.com/restaurant/), the revolving restaurant (one circuit every 47 minutes) now offers lunch and dinner menus that include starters such as braised elk tamales and a satay sampler, and entrees such as seared ahi tuna and Northwest sturgeon. Yes, prices are steep, and the restaurant has a dress code ('business casual attire'), but the food is pretty good. Besides, you have to eat somewhere, and dining here does include free access to the observation deck upstairs, assuming you spend the minimum per person, excluding alcohol.

Longtime Seattleites will often tell you that there are better places to get a view of the city, ranging from the area's tallest skyscraper (the Columbia Tower, which has an observation deck on its 73rd floor) to Queen Anne Hill, where the climb up the path is the only price you'll pay. Maybe. But no one back home will ask you about the best view, now will they? They'll want to know if you made it to the top of the Space Needle.

Right: the 'saucer on a stick' design was originally just a sketch on a napkin

6. FREMONT *(see map, p42)*

This tour discovers Fremont's funkiness, particularly its public art, as well as some fun eateries and a very different sort of public park.

Fremont is easily reached via a No. 17, 26 or 28 bus from Downtown (take the local, not the express bus). Get out on Nickerson, and walk across the Fremont Bridge.

The **Fremont Bridge**, built in 1917, opens as often as every ten minutes on a busy summer day to let through passing ships. Rather than express frustration, old-time Fremonteers celebrate this anti-bustle attitude with a sign exhorting visitors to 'set your watch back five minutes.' Welcome to Fremont.

The neighborhood was a busy industrial area from the 1890s through to the early 1930s, served by an interurban rail line and trolley cars. But the construction of the George Washington Bridge, high to the east of the neighborhood, marked the beginning of its decline. What was bad for industry was good for artists and eccentrics, however, who moved into the low-rent neighborhood and created a bohemian center, filled with musicians, students and like-minded people in love with an alternative lifestyle.

Since the 1960s, Fremont has done

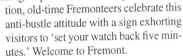

Above: *Waiting for the Interurban*
Left: draw bridges require a leisurely attitude

more than accept its eccentric nature: it has celebrated it. In the last few years, however, the neighborhood's coveted funkiness has begun to fade under the seemingly inevitable onslaught of high-tech gentrification. Local developers are hard at work transforming the run-down apartments and artists' lofts into condominiums and – well – artists' lofts.

Just after crossing the bridge, on the right, you'll see the biggest change the neighborhood has faced in recent years: software giant Adobe's massive office complex. Adobe displaced shops, bars and eateries, but some of their development has been positive. Like **Canal Park**, a pleasant green walk that runs alongside the **Fremont Canal**. Take the stairs down through the Adobe complex and head for the water for a pleasant stroll.

Cut up from the water at Evanston Avenue N and walk north to N 35th Street. Unmissable is the **Fremont Rocket**, a recycled relic from the Cold War. It's a noted and much-loved neighborhood site; whenever anyone familiar with the Pacific Northwest sees a photograph of the rocket, they almost automatically think 'Fremont.' Near the Rocket, and in several other locations around the neighborhood, you'll find **information kiosks** dispensing Fremont walking guides. They're free, so take one of these handy maps with you for further explorations. Continue one block north on Evanston. When you reach Fremont Place N, look across the street and you'll see a 16-ft (3.25-m) tall cast-bronze **Statue of Vladimir Lenin**.

This icon of the neighborhood was rescued from Slovakia by an entrepreneurial Seattleite after the fall of Communism.

Center of the Universe

Turn right down Fremont Place and you'll find yourself at the intersection of N 35th Street, Fremont Place N and Fremont Avenue N, at the curious and popular **'Center of the Universe' sign**. The different arms on the sign point out the various routes to local landmarks (like the Lenin statue a block back), as well as to more exotic locations such as the Louvre, Timbuktu and the Bermuda Triangle (in each case, spelling out how far every site is from Fremont's very own 'Center of the Universe').

Follow the arrow that points south and head one block down Fremont Avenue N to see *Waiting for the Interurban*. This popular piece of oddball art portrays a group of commuters waiting under a pergola for the arrival of a streetcar that stopped running in the 1930s. Depending on the season, mood or other events, the statues may be wearing parasols, mufflers or flags. If you instead turn north on Fremont Avenue N, in a half-block you'll reach **Empty Space** (3509 Fremont N, tel: 206 547-7500; www.emp-

Right: the Fremont Rocket is a recyled relic from the Cold War

tyspace.org), Seattle's venerable mid-sized theatre venue, which is a respected haven for new writing and experimental work.

Back at 'the Center,' you're within two blocks of several restaurants, bars and cafes with something for almost every appetite or budget. Choose Thai, Japanese or Greek, or turn into the aptly named Triangle Lounge (3507 Fremont Place N, tel: 206 632-0880), sandwiched between N 35th and Fremont Place N, which serves good bistro food in its small dining room and outdoor patio, and attracts a lively bar scene under a neon sign that reads 'Prescriptions.'

If you're craving something sweet, it's not far to Simply Desserts (3421 Fremont Avenue N, tel: 206 633-2671), where you can feast on fruit pie with ice cream, a gooey brownie or a slice of chocolate truffle cake.

Stroll past a Troll

Once refreshed, head east on N 35th Street and walk up the hill toward the underpass of the **Aurora Bridge** (also called the Washington Memorial Bridge). Turn left on Troll Avenue and you'll encounter a fearsome figure crouched a few dozen feet up, the *Fremont Troll*. This 15-ft (5-m) tall creature is made of concrete and clutches a real Volkswagon beetle in one hand. He presides over the neighborhood's annual Halloween celebration, 'Trolloween.' Fremont is known for its street festivities.

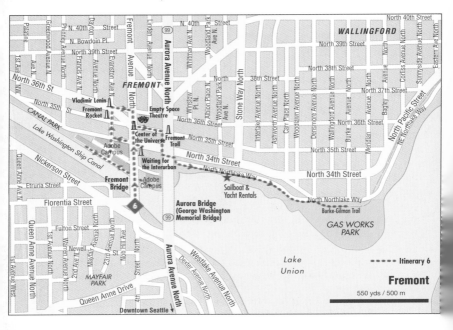

The annual Solstice Parade, held on the third Saturday in June (on or before the summer solstice), is a favorite with Seattleites. 2001 marked the 30th anniversary of the parade and the weekend-long Fremont Fair, where the community welcomes up to 100,000 visitors. Festival-goers gather to 'stroll, vend, move and groove, perform, eat, drink and celebrate the summer season.' It's also Seattle's largest crafts marketplace, with over 350 booths selling handmade goods. Live entertainment is a big feature, with five venues showcasing top local acts. There's a special stage along the ship canal so visitors can tune in to the music and watch sailboats float by at the same time. Concerts are often held in local watering holes to coincide with the outdoors entertainment. For more information about the Fremont Fair, *see page 79.*

Gas Works Park

Once you've enjoyed the *Fremont Troll*, turn around, walk down the underpass and cross the street. Descend to the lower walk beneath the sidewalk, which is a section of the lengthy **Burke-Gilman Trail**. Turn left and follow the trail. This is a pleasant walk near the shores of **Lake Union**, past yacht stores and a marina. Iin about ten blocks you'll emerge into **Gas Works Park**. If you want to carry on farther, Gas Works Park is the beginning of another section of the Burke-Gilman Trail *(see page 53).*

Heating and lighting gas had been manufactured here for half a century, then landscape architect Richard Haag was given the brief to design a public park on the site of a dilapidated gas works. His initial plan caused a scandal. Instead of leveling the old structure, he proposed a scheme incorporating much of the old plant, with the rusting structures rising above a rolling green expanse. The plan was approved after a great deal of local controversy, and the park that opened in 1975 has a frank vision of the consequences of man's industry. Retrace your path to Fremont Avenue N and take a bus back to Downtown, or head back to Fremont for shopping, dinner or drinks.

Left: the *Fremont Troll* presides over 'Trolloween,' Fremont's Halloween scene
Above: taking it easy in Gas Works Park

7. MUSEUM OF FLIGHT (see pull-out map)

Take a trip to the Northwest's largest air and space museum, then visit the bohemian neighborhood of Georgetown.

Jump on a No. 174 bus in downtown Seattle or rent a car and drive to the Museum of Flight.

Since the 1950s, Seattle has been known familiarly as 'Jet City' because of aircraft giant Boeing and the vast factory that produced passenger and military aircraft. In 2001, Boeing decided to move its headquarters to Chicago, and cut thousands of local jobs, so this high-flying nickname might fall out of favor. But interest in Boeing continues. The bus from Seattle drops passengers off right at the **Boeing factory**, and from here, it's just a short walk to the **Museum of Flight** at 9404 E Marginal Way S (daily 10am–5pm; Thur till 9pm; tel: 764-5720; www.museumofflight.org; admission fee). Although the museum takes pride in having the lovingly reconditioned **'Red Barn'** that was the first manufacturing facility of William Boeing's aeronautic empire, its relationship with the aerospace giant is entirely non-commercial.

There are more than 50 historic aircraft on display, pretty much what you'd expect from the Northwest's largest air and space museum. A Boeing 80A-1, built in 1929 and salvaged from a junkheap in Alaska, was the museum's first acquisition. The 737 is the most popular jetliner in the Boeing family; it was used by NASA as a research vehicle to test several technological innovations. There are also great exhibits on the design and production of early bi-planes and other prop aircraft. Some of the center's prize exhibits, like the Lockheed ***Blackbird***, the world's fastest plane, include full-size models of the cockpit and engine. The museum's most impressive possession is the permanently docked ***Air Force One***, the famous aircraft used by presidents Eisenhower, Kennedy, Johnson and Nixon.

If you've come by car or don't mind taking a different bus route back (changing at E Marginal Way from the 174 to the 131 or 134), consider visiting the **Georgetown** neighborhood, an area that some say actually pre-

dates both Alki and Seattle as the first white – as opposed to Native American – settlement in King County.

In its early years Georgetown had many different incarnations, including hop fields; as a ramshackle collection of shady saloons and brothels; and as a partner with Boeing, which began with the building of a major plant in 1935.

Now the area is beginning to shed its industrial identity for a new one, as derelict factories, warehouses and other buildings are taken over by artists, writers, musicians and assorted bohemian malcontents. One of the businesses to move into the neighborhood has been local coffee giant Tully's, who have turned the Rainier Brewing Plant into a Roasting Plant, and replaced the signature red 'R' on the factory with a green 'T.'

The result of this new influx is a couple of funky and stylish streets, very possibly the beginning of a full-fledged renaissance for Georgetown. Particularly recommended are the coffee, gallery space and theatre at All City Coffee (1205 S Vale Street, tel: 206 767-7146). Just around the corner, Big People Scooters (5951 Airport Way S, tel: 206 763-0160; www.bigpeoplescooters.com), is a store for new and beautifully reconditioned scooters and Vespas.

8. MUSEUM OF HISTORY AND INDUSTRY *(see map, p46)*

An absorbing museum of Seattle's history and a ramble through large and varied parks. Wear a pair of comfortable shoes.

Take a No. 43 bus from Downtown to the intersection of Montlake Boulevard E and E Hamlin Street. Turn right on Hamlin and walk three blocks to the Museum of History and Industry (MOHAI).

Don't be put off by the name. **The Museum of History and Industry** (MOHAI; 2700 24th Avenue E; daily 10am–5pm; tel: 324-1126, www.seattlehistory.org; admission fee) is definitely worth a visit, particularly for the Metropolis 150 exhibit, a celebration of Seattle's first 150 years. Make this excellent 'city history primer' your first stop; the displays cleverly bring together archive photos, film and artifacts ranging from the 'Petticoat Stars and Stripes' that flew during the one-day Indian War in 1856, to relics from such short-lived web businesses as Kozmo.com.

The museum's focus on how businesses and industry have developed the spirit and character of Seattle is a refreshing approach to history. There are

Above left: this bust guards Boeing's 'Little Red Barn.' **Left:** the Museum of Flight
Above: Georgetown, a bohemian neighborhood in the making

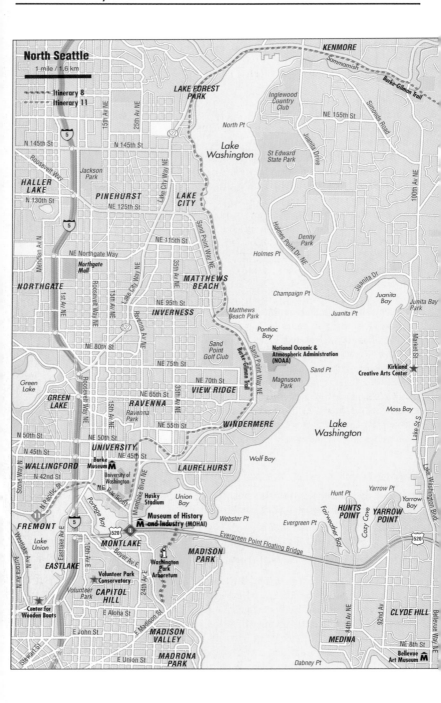

North Seattle

1 mile / 1.6 km

- - - Itinerary 8
- - - Itinerary 11

also exhibits that kids especially enjoy, including a periscope that shows how the landscape has changed from what the first settlers saw, and an ongoing display called 'Salmon Stakes' that gives them a chance to see what canning fish on a 'slime line' is like.

There are plans to move MOHAI to Downtown. While the move would be good, encouraging more tourists to visit, it would be a shame to lose the current site close to the **Arboretum**, an astonishingly diverse park.

In the Arboretum

'Parks' might be a better description than merely 'park.' The arboretum is huge and varied; you could spend days exploring it. It dates back to 1924, when local gardeners suggested an experiment to the University of Washington to learn which plants from around the world could thrive in the region's rich soil and temperate climate. The Federal government later added sponsorship; now the arboretum is co-managed by the University of Washington and the City of Seattle.

The result is over 5,500 plant species flourishing in the 230-acre (93-hectare) area, producing explosions of color every season. Cherries and azaleas blossom in the spring, dogwoods and magnolias bloom in summer, the leaves of the birch and mountain ash turn in the fall, and the festive holly sprays red and deep green in winter. Detailed guide books to this part of the park are available from the museum's front desk.

Enter the park at the far end of the parking lot by the entrance. This first section is a preserved marsh area with floating walkways. Take the path to the right, looking out for the birds that frequent the area, such as the Marsh wren, goldfinches, mallards, Virginia rails and Canada geese.

A footbridge leads from **Marsh Island** to **Foster Island**. Pass the arboretum work yard and turn left at Arboretum Drive E, then go uphill to the **Graham Visitors Center** (2300 Arboretum Drive E, tel: 206 543-8800; www.depts.washington.edu/wpa/) and pick up a free map. The bookstore is well worth browsing while you're here.

Be sure to visit the fine **Japanese Garden** (telephone: 206 684-4725; www.seattlejapanesegarden.org; pay a small admission fee). Created by master gardener Juki Iida, it is a recreation of a traditional meditation garden. The garden includes a lake stocked with *koi*, water lilies, a cherry orchard and a Tea Garden.

If you've worked up an appetite and would like to explore the interesting but pricey neighborhood of **Madison Park** just outside the arboretum, consider finishing with a dinner of sushi at Nishimo (3130 E Madison, tel: 206 322-5800).

Right: figurehead exhibit from MOHAI

9. WOODLAND PARK
AND GREEN LAKE *(see map, p50)*

An award-winning zoo, and a trip to Seattle's most popular park. Much of this tour is on foot, so wear appropriate shoes.

Take a No. 5 bus from Downtown, heading to Phinney Ridge. Get off at Phinney Avenue N and 49th. Walk up to 50th, and take a right. Three blocks along you're at the southern entrance of the Woodland Park Zoo. If you're driving, there is paid parking at the zoo's north and south entrances.

In 1889, developer Guy Phinney had a 179 acre (72-hectare) estate that centered around a lake – and equally big plans. He built a hotel, a bandstand and a ballpark around the lake and even a streetcar line in order to lure people to buy parcels of land. He added a menagerie and a rose garden, but economic depression and Phinney's early death left the project incomplete. In 1895 the city bought the estate, including the zoo, from his widow.

Since the days of Phinney, the **Woodland Park Zoo** (daily 9.30am–6pm, 4pm in winter; 5500 Phinney Avenue N, tel: 206 684-4800; www.zoo.org; admission fee) has seen many changes. Most of these have been for the better, for both animals and visitors. Since 1977 the park has been renovated, creating environments similar to the animals' homes in the wild. Miniature savannas, a rainforest and an elephant forest offer much more space to the zoo's inhabitants.

As a result, some of the animals – like the big cats – aren't always to be seen, but they look happy when you *do* see them. For the best chance of seeing the animals, go in the morning. Even people who are depressed by creatures in cap-

tivity can see that life in Woodland ain't so bad.

Coming out at the south entrance (where you came in), turn left and stroll across the parking lot to the **Woodland Park Rose Garden**. Phinney's original plan has been developed into magnificent beds for dozens of different rose varieties, some of which bloom late into the autumn. Wander among beautiful flowers with names like 'Singin' in the Rain,' 'Esmeralda' or even 'Reba McIntyre.'

The People's Park

Leaving the Rose Garden through the back, or northern exit, you'll walk along a driveway curving to the right, down to the Zoo Maintenance area. At certain times of the year 'Zoo Doo' from a variety of the menagerie's inhabitants is avail-

Left: October colors in the city

able for gardening enthusiasts. Follow the sign to 'Green Lake' down the underpass for a while, then across the concrete overpass that spans Aurora. Now you're in **Woodland Park**, green and serene, with picnic areas, lawns and shaded tree-lined walks. To get to **Green Lake Park**, take a left and walk along the path past two other overpasses, then down to the parking lot. Follow the drive that curves down from the parking lot, and you'll be across the street from one of the most pleasant – but busiest – recreational places in the city.

Green Lake

The waters of **Green Lake** ripple against grassy shores in the middle of the high-density neighborhood of the same name. It's a lake in a city surrounded by water, an algae-tinged reservoir born of glacial gougings 50,000 years ago. The lake was first 'settled' by Erhart Seifried in 1869, and was very different from what exists now. As part of their creation of the parks system of Seattle, the Olmsted Brothers planned to lower the lake by 7ft (2m). Much land was reclaimed from swamp, but an unforeseen consequence was to cut off the lake from its source of fresh water, resulting in massive amounts of algae. Treatments and dredging have helped ease this problem, but swimming is still at your own risk, as algae can cause uncomfortable 'swimmer's itch.'

Most of the activity on the lake is on the 2.8-mile (4.5-km) **waterside trail**. This wide paved lane is marked

Above: Woodland Park Rose Garden
Right: Woodland Park Zoo weathervane

one side for wheels, and the other for feet. Runners often stick to the crushed gravel that forms a third lane on the inside. Joggers, bikers, strollers, dog-walkers and skaters proceed in what's an odd combination of exercise and promenade. Tennis courts, soccer, baseball and boat rentals are all options, as

is fishing from the docks or picnicking. Rent a pair of blades or admire the ducks at the waterfowl sanctuary; also be on the look-out for the resident great heron. Green Lake is undeniably a 'scene' in that laidback way so familiar to the Northwest. It's common for a first date to include a stroll along the path, which is guaranteed to suit or soothe divergent tastes, as it combines fine scenery and a closeness to nature with lots of good people-watching.

Lakeside dining

If you're feeling energetic, you can stroll all the way round the lake; if not, just take in that part that suits you, stopping off along the way at one of the cafés and restaurants across the street from the lake. Eateries range from trendy watering holes to fish and chip places. When you're ready to head back, return the way you came, or catch a No. 16 or 26 bus on Ravenna Boulevard NE near E Green Lake Drive N. This will take you directly back to Downtown.

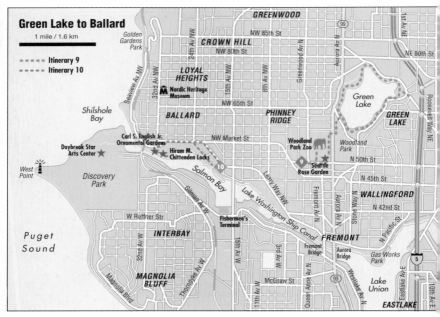

Green Lake to Ballard

10. BALLARD (SEE MAP, P50)

Visit Seattle's funky-in-the-making neighborhood of musicians, artists, hipsters and Norwegians. It's a fun and funny place undergoing a quiet culture clash.

Take the No. 15 bus from Downtown to 15th and NW Market Street, or the No. 18 bus to Ballard Avenue NW and NW Market Street. If you've taken the No. 15, turn west and continue down Market till you get to 20th. Take a left on 20th, passing the Swedish Medical Center, and continuing to Ballard Avenue NW. If you took the No. 18, turn south down Ballard Avenue NW.

If the funkiness is leaking out of Fremont *(see page 40)*, **Ballard** is where it's headed. For decades this has been a sleepy and conservative neighborhood, whose greatest pride has been in its fishing fleet and its Norwegian heritage. Local stores specialized in 'delicacies' such as *lutefisk* and *lefse*. While there are still plenty of senior citizens and sleepy streets in Ballard, there are also coffee shops, bars, restaurants and places that are positively hopping of an evening. This funny and fun neighborhood is undergoing a quiet culture clash.

Shilshole Avenue NW and Ballard Avenue NW run parallel to each other for a few blocks here, with funky stores and restaurant-bars that turn into live music clubs at nighttime. Cross back and forth between these two streets and enjoy the old Ballard storefronts, carpentry stores and bait shops amid the new boutiques and wine bars.

For a place where the residents of young and old Ballard eat and drink together, cross up to **Hattie's Hat** (5231 Ballard Avenue NW, tel: 206 784-0175; www.hattieshat.com). The first thing you notice in the dark interior is the bar on your left, which has been here since the bar-restaurant first opened in 1902, several name-changes ago. The food's traditional American diner: meatloaf sandwiches or tuna melts, but served with sass. Hattie's is

Left: rent rollerblades, play tennis or just go fishing in Green Lake
Above: the Hiram M Chittenden Locks link the lakes with Puget Sound

a great place to meet Ballard on its own eccentric terms. Like neighboring Fremont, Ballard has been seeing an influx of trendy restaurants and beautiful people lately. The latter congregate at the former, including Matador (2221 NW Market, tel: 206 297-2855) and the Portalis wine bar (5310 Ballard Avenue NW, tel: 206 783-2007).

When you have eventually finished window-shopping or chatting with the folks at Hattie's or another diner, continue up the street toward NW Market Street. Take a left on Market and watch out for a giant dragon head looming out of one of the walls. This is **Archie McPhee & Co** (2428 NW Market Street, tel: 206 297-0240; www.mcphee.com) The interior of this entirely original store looks as though a South Seas trading outpost was overcome, not by angry Natives but by the world's largest collection of gadgets, gewgaws and other eccentricities.

After the wonderful tackiness of Archie's, continue down Market till you come to NW 54th Street. Take a left down this street and walk for about a block to the entrance of the **Hiram M Chittenden Locks** (daily 7am–9pm; free). This is a delightful working lock system which links lakes Washington and Union to Puget Sound. Completed in 1917, the locks allow vessels to travel between the freshwater lakes and the saltwater bay. Roughly 80,000 vessels use the lock each year, so you'll almost certainly get to watch the locks in action. The officials raise or lower the water level from 6 to 26ft (2–8m), according to the tides. Alongside this engineering marvel, there's a small **visitors' center** (10am–4 or 6pm, depending on season, closed

Tues–Wed except in summer; tel: 206 783-7059) telling the story of the locks, and 8 acres (3.2 hectares) of **botanical gardens**, where live events are occasionally held. There's a **fish ladder**, which allows salmon to navigate through the waterways, and an underground fish-viewing window, where you can watch them surging to their rendezvous with destiny. June and July are the spawning season.

If you have an appetite for more education, walk a few blocks up to the **Nordic Heritage Museum** (3014 67th Street NW; Tues–Sat 10am–4pm, Sun noon–4pm, closed Mon; tel: 206 789-5707; www.nordicmuseum.org; admission fee). Exhibits here chart the stories of the neighborhood's original settlers, whose culture and temperament were such a major influence on Seattle's history.

If you'd like to stay in Ballard for the evening, you can easily satisfy cravings for fish 'n' chips or diner food. If you'd like something more elegant, try the Market Street Grill (see 'Eating Out,' page 73). Or, if you'd prefer to end your evening with some of the live music that's fast becoming Ballard's big draw, try the funky Tractor Tavern (5213 Ballard Avenue NW, tel: 206 789-3599; www.tractortavern.com) for rockabilly, or the Old Town Alehouse (5233 Ballard NW, tel: 206 782-8323) for jazz, or the Conor Byrne Pub (5140 Ballard NW, tel: 206 784-3640) for traditional Irish music.

11. THE BURKE-GILMAN TRAIL *(see map, p46)*

Hike, bike or skate along a disused railroad line.

You can join the trail anywhere along its route; call the Seattle Bicycle Program, tel: 206 684-7583 for a map. Nearby bike rentals are listed here.

The **Burke-Gilman Trail** runs along the lines of a disused railroad, the Seattle, Lake Shore and Eastern, and is a sterling example of the 'rails to trails' movement. You can join the trail anywhere along its route, though the most popular starting places are near **Gas Works Park** (see page 43) or on the **University of Washington** college campus.

The best part of the trail is beyond Sand Point Way NE, where it hugs the banks of Lake Washington, offering a series of gorgeous vistas and plenty of flat land, which is perfect if you're on a bike. If you ride to **Kenmore's Log Boom Park** and want to keep going, you can link up to the **Sammamish River Trail**, which continues 13 miles (21km) more to **Lake Sammamish** on the Eastside. It passes through 33 acres (13.3 hectares) of wetlands that contain fascinating wildlife. At the end of the trail is **Marymoor Park**, which has the

Above Left: Seattle stroll. **Left:** botanic magic **Right:** Gas Works Park

only velodrome (a sports arena equipped with a banked track for cycling) in the Pacific Northwest. You have to be a trained rider to use the facility, but classes are offered; call the Bike Hotline for details. Plans are underway to link up the trail with another derelict rail line, which would extend the bike path still farther.

A note of caution: there are a few places where the trail runs near to automobile traffic. More than a few accidents have resulted, particularly near Gas Works Park and near the University of Washington. Minimize risk to yourself and other trail users by observing the 15 mph (24 kph) speed limit.

Here are a few addresses of **bike rentals** located fairly near the trail: All About Bike and Ski, 3615 NE 45th, tel: 206 524-2642, www.allaboutbikeandski.com; The Bicycle Center, 4529 Sand Point Way NE, tel: 206 523-8300, www.bicyclecenterseattle.com; Gregg's Green Lake Cycle, 7007 Woodland Avenue NE, tel: 206 523-1822, www.greggscycles.com. These shops also have maps, and know the trail well.

12. WEST SEATTLE   *(see map, p56)*

A brief ride across Puget Sound to West Seattle and the origins of the modern city, then a leisurely walk along the waterfront. Take a jacket as the wind off the water can be stiff, even in the summertime.

In summertime, take the Elliott Bay Water Taxi (tel: 553-3000, http://transit.metrokc.gov/) from Pier 54 at the Seattle waterfront. In the off-season, take a No. 37 bus from Downtown directly to West Seattle's Alki Beach, getting near 61st SW and Alki Avenue SW, and picking up our tour there.

A water taxi ride is the most glamorous way to get to West Seattle, as it's fun to twist backward in the boat and watch the skyscrapers of the city recede into the background. If you've taken the bus, **Seacrest Park** isn't much of a place to linger, so when you arrive, go to Harbor Avenue SW, turn right and start walking to the more scenic parts of this tour. Alternatively, wait for a shuttle bus and hop off at Alki Beach.

Above: rent a bike and hit the Burke-Gilman Trail
Right: Statue of Liberty replica, Alki Beach

If you're walking, you've got a pleasant stroll ahead, along the waterfront. There are still a few older cottages to your left, though many of the views are now dominated by expensive condominiums. Continue along the avenue for about a third of a mile and you come to **Duwamish Head**, the tip of the West Seattle peninsula. This viewpoint is definitely worth a stop. There are 'viewers' set up here, and through them you'll see historical vignettes from West Seattle's early days.

Alki Beach

Harbor Avenue SW turns into Alki Avenue SW after Duwamish Head. Soon you'll find yourself on **Alki Beach**. If it's sunny, there's bound to be a beach crowd playing on the sand and enjoying themselves.

Some commentators refer to Alki's summer scene as 'a little bit of California,' and it's true that you'll see hardy Seattleites sunbathing and playing volleyball on the wide sandy stretch past Bonair Drive SW. Breezes across the chilly saltwater of Puget Sound tend to deter tourists from donning bikinis, however. It's a pleasant place for a stroll though, with restaurants and bars, plus houses and condos that have enviable views. During the summer, you can also rent bikes or in-line skates.

You get a wonderful view of Seattle's skyline here, one that would have flabbergasted those early settlers back in 1851. Commemorative markers set along the beach pay tribute, not only to the Denny Party, but to the Native Americans who lived here before them. Near 61st Avenue SW is an incongruous miniature replica of the **Statue of Liberty**. This was donated to the city in 1952, in echo of the settlement's first name, 'New York Alki.'

For more on Seattle's history, turn left onto 61st Avenue SW and follow it for about a block until it intersects Stevens Street. On your right-hand side is the **Log House Museum** (Thur–Sun limited hours; tel: 206 938-5293; www.loghousemuseum.org; by donation) which houses a small exhibit on West Seattle's meaning to the Native people and their life here, in addi-

bove: beach bistro for lunch, dinner and seafood

tion to the area's growth as a neighborhood. The **Birthplace of Seattle obelisk**, presented to the city in 1905, is two blocks down from here near Alki Avenue SW and 63rd Avenue SW.

The **Alki Point Lighthouse** (summer weekends noon–4pm; tel: 206 217-6124) is five blocks along Alki Avenue, at the western point of the peninsula. The lighthouse, established in 1881 (the present lighthouse was built in 1913), offers an evocative view of the sea and surroundings.

Old-Growth Forest

Small but distinctive **Schmitz Park** is not far away. Turn left from the lighthouse and start up SW Admiral Way, which is a steady climb for several blocks. Your goal is about ten blocks along on your right. This ancient land was deeded to the city of Seattle on condition that it be kept in its original state, making it one of the few remaining stands of old-growth forest in the city. Paths meander through land virtually unchanged from that which greeted settlers 150 years ago. From Schmitz Park, return to Alki Avenue via Stevens Street, then turn right on 57th Avenue SW. Catch a No. 37 bus on Alki Avenue SW for a ride back to Downtown. Alternately, you can grab a shuttle back to Seacrest or retrace your steps, and catch the water taxi back to downtown Seattle.

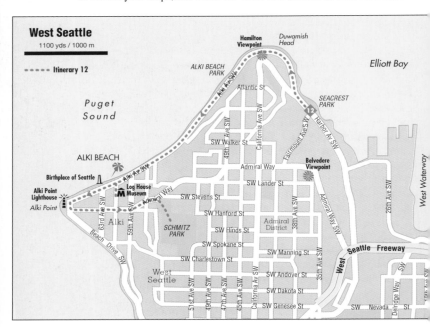

13. THE THEATRE SCENE (SEE PULL-OUT MAP)

In Seattle you can see a different production almost every night of the week, from vaudeville to drama to traveling musicals. Note that on Mondays, theatres are traditionally dark.

Buy tickets direct from the box office, to save paying Ticketmaster's handling fees. Even better is Ticket/Ticket, tel: 206 324-2744, which operates one kiosk next to the Market Information booth in the Pike Place Market, and another in Capitol Hill's Broadway Market at 401 Broadway Avenue E. These booths offer same-day tickets for half the original box-office price, and seats are usually very good.

Seattle is a big theatre town; in America, only LA and New York claim to have more productions. The 'Seattle Style' of performance is hard to define, but it's typically characterized by broad and quick comedy, smart and versatile actors, and a surprising fondness for vaudevillian novelty acts. Fringe theatre often yields the best value for your dollar. For specific show listings, check out the free weeklies, the *Seattle Weekly* and *The Stranger*. In typical laid-back Northwest fashion, audiences either dress up smart in their glad-rags or stay casual; either style will do.

A Long History

Washington's theatre roots stretch back to its early days, when two local impresarios set up a series of theatres in the 1880s and 1890s. John Considine, who ran the nation's first vaudeville circuit, had theatres stretching from Victoria to Portland. His chief competitor, Alexander Pantages, was an energetic young Greek who'd returned from the Alaskan goldfields, where he'd made his money not with a gold pan but with a playhouse.

Pantages also got well into the circuit-building business, and soon the pair had houses that stretched up and down the West Coast, with the zeal to bring singers, dancers, comedians, animal performers and others to their theatres.

The **Moore Theatre**, a beautifully faded old building constructed in 1907 and located downtown at Second Avenue and Spring, is one of the few reminders of those glory days of the vaudeville circuits. In the 1960s, several theatres, including the Seattle Rep, Intiman and ACT, were founded, along with the **Empty Space**, the eccentric grandfather of the current crop of fringe and alternative theatres.

In the mid-1990s, thanks to the national media, Seattle's theatre scene was vast to the point of unwieldy. Not only Equity theatres but also mid-sized houses and a number of smaller or 'fringe' companies

Left: the Alki Point Lighthouse
Right: buy/buy from a Ticket/Ticket kiosk

filled every available space year round. These days there's less theatre, but the quality has matured and often improved beyond anything that went before it.

Seattle's major theatres are the Seattle Repertory Theatre, Intiman, ACT and the Seattle Children's Theatre. The **5th Avenue Theatre** presents a mixture of locally produced musicals and truck shows, while the **Paramount** and Moore theatres produce almost exclusively traveling companies. On the Boards presents more eclectic theatrical and dance companies who stop in Seattle while touring around the world.

Theater Schmeater

There are a number of 'mid-sized' houses featuring professional productions in more intimate settings; these include The Empty Space, Taproot Theatre, ArtsWest, Book-It and Seattle Shakespeare Company. Finally, there are dozens of fringe theatre companies, which produce shows throughout the year, including Open Circle, Theater Schmeater and Seattle Public Theatre, which have their own venues, and Annex, Theatre Simple, House of Dames and other companies, which rent spaces as required.

While there are community theatres throughout Puget Sound and the occasional professional house off the beaten path (like the Space in Fremont or Taproot in the Greenwood area), the greatest concentration of theatres in the immediate Seattle area can be found in two very different 'districts,' the first-rate but slightly sterile Seattle Center, and the lighter, more bohemian Capitol Hill area.

Seattle Center Area

The **Seattle Repertory Theatre** (tel: 206 443-2222; www.seattlerep.org) has two theatres, the Bagley Wright and the Leo K. and plays a mix of classics and standard regional favorites. **Intiman** (tel: 206 269-1900; www.intiman.org) has returned to its roots and specializes in remounted classics. The **Seattle Children's Theatre** (tel: 206 441-3322; www.sct.org) is a nationally recognized venue for intelligent work for children and teenagers. It also has two separate stages.

Slightly hidden in the basement of Center House are two of Seattle's mid-sized theatres, **Seattle Shakespeare** (206 tel: 733-8222; www.seattleshakespeare.org) and **Book-It** (tel: 206 216-0833, www.book-it.org), which specialize respectively in works of the Bard and adaptations of classic literature. Near the Seattle Center in nearby **Queen Anne** is **On the Boards** (100 W Roy, tel: 206 217-9888; www.ontheboards.org), the city's home for progressive and eclectic dance and theatre.

Capitol Hill Area

At the dividing line between Downtown and Capitol Hill are two of Seattle's largest theatres, **ACT** (700 Union, tel: 206 292-7676; www.acttheatre.org), and the **Paramount** (900 Pine, 9th Avenue and Pine, tel: 292-ARTS). Both are housed in vintage buildings that have received resplendent renovations, with perhaps the prize going to ACT, which has turned the former world

headquarters for the Eagles Fraternal Lodge into a four-space theatre complex. ACT's devotion to new works and innovative programming have made it one of the most consistently interesting theatres in this part of the Northwest.

The scene in Capitol Hill proper is scrappier and often more intriguing. **Theater Schmeater** (1500 Summit, tel: 206 324-5801; www.schmeater.org), housed in a former parking garage, offers a fun mix of serious work and goofball late-night shows. Other venues are **Hugo House** (1634 11th Avenue, tel: 206 322-7030; www.hugohouse.org), a center for writers, which also has a theatre used by several companies. **Freehold** (1529 10th Avenue, tel: 206 323-7499) and the **Northwest Actor's Studio** (1100 E Pike Street, tel: 206 323-6300; www.nwactorsstudio.org) are theatre schools where facilities are often rented by various companies. Some companies have migrated: **Seattle Public Theater** (tel: 206 524-1300; www.seattlepublictheater.org) stages shows in the old bathhouse at Green Lake, and **Live Girls!** (2220 NW Market Street, tel: 800-838-3006; www.livegirlstheater.org), featuring work by women playwrights, is in Ballard.

Above Left: show lists are found in weekly papers. **Left:** Theater Schmeater foyer
Right: Washington's theatre roots stretch back to the 1880s

Excursions

1. SNOQUALMIE AND NORTH BEND
(see map, p62)

This excursion takes in a sample of the mountainous and spectacular scenery that lies to the east of Seattle, including a huge waterfall, a rail-road museum and a small town made famous by TV's *Twin Peaks*.

A car is required for this trip. Snoqualmie is located about 45 minutes from downtown Seattle, traffic permitting.

From Interstate 90 heading east, take the Snoqualmie Exit #27. Take a left under the freeway and follow the posted signs to Snoqualmie and Snoqualmie Falls. Turn left after about ½ mile, travel another ½ mile, and turn left again at the stop sign. The falls are about a mile (2km) farther along. This entire route is well marked. Quicker but much less scenic is to cut through Snoqualmie Parkway, a nearby suburban development.

Sacred Waterfalls

The **Snoqualmie Falls** are sacred to the local Native Americans. They attribute their creation to Snoqualm, the Moon God, who transformed a fish trap into the falls in the hope of allowing salmon to swim upstream. It would take a mighty leap indeed for a fish to make it up the falls; at 276ft (84m) in height, Snoqualmie is 109ft (930m) taller than Niagara.

The first white explorer to see the falls was Washington Hall, a surveyor who was led to the site by Natives in 1848. By 1865, groups of tourists were traveling to the falls from Seattle, and in 1889, a rail-line opened in nearby North Bend, the same year that famed naturalist John Muir visited. Engineer Charles H Baker was impressed by the potential for turbine power at the falls, and convinced his wealthy father to pay for a power plant. In 1899, work was completed on an innovative design, using a huge pipe to the side of the main falls linked to four turbines in a subterranean chamber, harnessing the falls' power, but remaining out of view. 32,000 volts of electricity were produced and, over a hundred years later, the plant is still in operation.

The hotel at the top of the falls is the **Salish Lodge**, a luxury inn with a spa and an award-winning restaurant *(see accommodation, page 88, for details.)* The prices are steep but the view of the falls from the dining room is spectacular, and the weekend brunches are justifiably famous.

An observation deck for the falls was built in 1968 and the most dramatic views to be had from it are during the spring thaws or after any heavy rain, when the spray from the

Left: Snoqualmie Falls
Right: there's something fishy about this paint job

water cascading into the river below rises majestically, and the impact of the crashing falls is immense. However, the effect at any time is spectacular.

Snoqualmie Falls has two small towns nearby, the tiny town of Snoqualmie, and the neighboring community of North Bend. **Snoqualmie**, less than a half mile from the falls, had a population of 1,500 for many years. But with the recent demand for housing close to Seattle, it has swelled to 6,300 and will probably keep growing.

For the time being, however, Snoqualmie is still a sweet little town with a few antiques stores and the **Northwest Railway Museum** (38625 SE King Street, Snoqualmie, tel: 425 888-3030; www.trainmuseum.org), located at the left of the intersection with King Street. A small, working depot houses a library and exhibits, while in the train yards next to the station are a number of antique steam trains, including several that are operational. One of the popular activities that the museum offers are regular rides from Snoqualmie to North Bend along 5 miles (8km) of active track.

North Bend, population 4,700, is located a few miles southeast of Snoqualmie. It is easily reached via the SE Snoqualmie–North Bend Road, which runs from downtown Snoqualmie directly to the heart of its neighboring community, which is surprisingly well known.

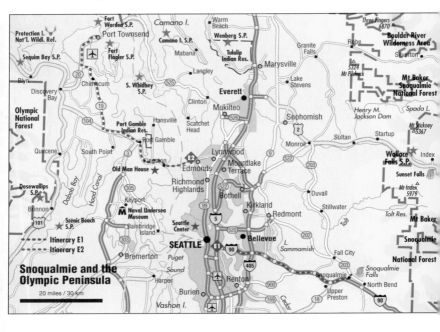

North Bend's fame comes from the 1990s cult TV show *Twin Peaks*, parts of which were filmed in the area. More than a decade on, the town still has visitors who are thrilled to see locations from the show. 'Peak Freaks' often stop at **Twedes Café** (tel: 425-831-5511), which appeared on the show as the Double R Diner. The years have brought changes, but they still serve 'a damn fine cherry pie,' and coffee 'black as midnight on a moonless night.' It's too tidy a place to qualify as a greasy spoon, but it's better for a snack than for a main meal.

Most visitors now come for the somewhat incongruous activities of hiking (especially climbing towering **Mount Si**) and shopping (at the factory stores at **North Bend outlet mall**). Downtown, there's a small and sweetly overstuffed antiques store, Bad Girl Antiques (42901 SE North Bend Way, tel: 425-888-1902). Time, then, to return to Seattle, perhaps snatching a second look at the falls on the way back, and enjoying the drive through pretty Northwest woods.

2. THE OLYMPIC PENINSULA
AND PORT TOWNSEND *(see maps, p62 and 64)*

A ferry ride and a visit to an historic city via some stunning scenery.

This tour requires a car and some planning; call Washington State Ferries, tel: 206 464-6400 for a schedule. If you intend to stay overnight, book a room from one of the choices listed here. Start from Edmonds, north of Seattle – take Interstate 5 going north. Then take the Edmonds–Kingston ferry exit.

Over the short distance of this trip you will experience surprising changes. Only a few miles west of Seattle are thick forests and extreme weather conditions. The cause is the Olympic mountain range, which divides up the precipitation. Forks, a town on the southern coast, receives 140in (355cm) of rain a year, while Sequim, a farming town in the Dungeness Valley near Port Townsend, gets less than 20in (51cm) a year.

Left: engine power at Snoqualmie's Northwest Railway Museum
Above: a 'Peak Freak,' a fan of TV's *Twin Peaks*, savors 'damn fine cherry pie'

The Edmonds Ferry is a quick, scenic jaunt across **Puget Sound** to the tiny town of **Kingston**, located on the eastern coast of Kitsap County. If you didn't have time to eat breakfast before you left Seattle, there are several cafés in Kingston serving hardy meals.

From Kingston, take the 104 heading west toward **Port Gamble**. If there's time, this attractive town, with its New England atmosphere, is worth a detour before you cross the bridge over the **Hood Canal**; it was founded in the 1850s by two families from Maine.

The **Hood Canal Bridge** is a floating bridge, one of the longest in the world at 1½ miles (2.5km), and crosses tidal waters. The view on either side of the bridge is awe-inspiring. Take 104, then take the Chimacum Road 19 to the north. This will lead to Port Townsend, which is about 5 miles (8km) farther along.

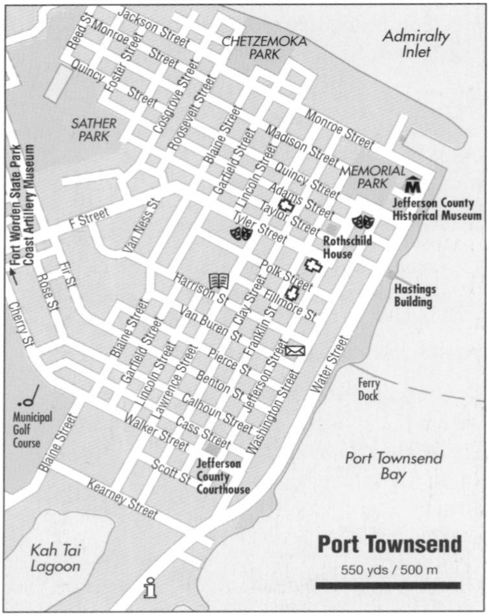

Port Townsend is a town that most developers, if not time, forgot. Founded the same year as Seattle, its beautiful setting and good harborage led early settlers to call it 'the City of Dreams.' But when the railroad bosses chose Tacoma, the town south of Seattle, over Port Townsend as their terminus,

*Map labels: Jackson Street, Monroe Street, CHETZEMOKA PARK, Admiralty Inlet, Reed St, Quincy Street, Foster Street, Cosgrove Street, SATHER PARK, Roosevelt Street, Blaine Street, Madison Street, Monroe Street, Garfield Street, Lincoln Street, Quincy Street, Adams Street, MEMORIAL PARK, Jefferson County Historical Museum, Fort Worden State Park Coast Artillery Museum, F Street, Van Ness Street, Taylor Street, Tyler Street, Rothschild House, First St, Rosa St, Harrison Street, Polk Street, Fillmore St, Hastings Building, Cherry St, Blaine Street, Van Buren St, Clay Street, Franklin St, Garfield Street, Lincoln Street, Lawrence Street, Pierce St, Benton St, Jefferson Street, Washington Street, Water Street, Ferry Dock, Municipal Golf Course, Blaine Street, Calhoun Street, Cass Street, Walker Street, Scott St, Jefferson County Courthouse, Port Townsend Bay, Kearney Street, Kah Tai Lagoon, **Port Townsend**, 550 yds / 500 m*

Above: a sailor's beacon

the set back had a lasting effect. Port Townsend's short-lived boom was over by 1890, leaving the lovely Victorian houses and formerly hard-working residents and businesses stranded in a depressed economy.

Historic houses

Many of these houses have been turned into bed-and-breakfast inns, which makes the town popular as a place to stay overnight. If this idea appeals to you, here are a few recommendations: the **Ann Starrett Mansion** (744 Clay Street, tel: 360 385-3205; www.starrettmansion.com; moderate–expensive) is a vast historic landmark, a magnificent Victorian house with daily tours, a grand spiral staircase and museum-quality antiques in the rooms. The **James House** (1238 Washington Street, tel: 360 385-1238; www.jameshouse.com; moderate–expensive) claims to be the Northwest's first bed-and-breakfast inn. Whatever the case, it certainly is luxurious, and the view of the waterfront is sumptuous. The **Ravenscroft Inn** (533 Quincy Street, tel: 360 385-2784; www.ravenscroftinn.com; moderate) is a pleasant though modern building with a welcoming hostess and tasty breakfasts.

Water Street and **Washington Street** contain most of Port Townsend's art galleries (gallery walks are held on the first Saturday of every month), as well as many boutiques and shops. At the north end of Water Street is a marina and several maritime-based industries. **St Paul's Church**, with its fire-engine-red door, is well worth taking a peek inside.

This cheerful community, with its unrivaled scenery, is happy to have tourists in their midst and there are plenty of watering holes. If you're after a tempting nibble, drop by the Tyler Street Bakery (215 Tyler Street, tel: 360 379-4185) and try the yummy cookies.

After wandering around the cozy, scenic streets, consider a quick visit to **Fort Worden State Park**, a large (434-acre/175-hectare) park that adjoins Port Townsend to the northeast. Fort Worden was part of a defensive network built during the 1880s. Now a state park and conference center, the installation is also the home of the **Coast Artillery Museum** (summer 11am–4pm, tel: 360-344-4454; admission fee).

Overnight stays are available in restored officers' homes on the south side (tel: 360 344-4400 or 800 360-4240; www.fortworden.org; moderate–expensive), as well as in a local hostel (tel: 360 385-0655; inexpensive) that is not far away.

ght: the Ann Starrett Mansion

Leisure Activities

SHOPPING

Seattle has an outstanding mix of small boutiques, home-grown retail giants like Nordstrom and Eddie Bauer, and the sort of national and international chains you'd expect in a major city. The three main shopping areas are Downtown, Capitol Hill and Fremont, and they've been divided here, when appropriate, into Inexpensive, Reasonable and Expensive.

Downtown, Inexpensive

You have a few dollars in your pocket and you'd like to leave Seattle with something more than an empty Starbucks paper cup? For everything from $1.99 socks to discount shoes and bedding, **Ross Dress for Less** (301 Pike Street, tel: 206 623-6781) is downtown Seattle's best department store choice. You'll have a lot to sort through on two floors, but take the time to do this, as it's almost always worth it for the bargains.

Local mega-retailer Nordstrom (stores are located all over the United States, but the company started here in 1901, opening a shoe shop in downtown Seattle) made sales-sensitive shoppers very happy with the arrival of their **Nordstrom Rack** (1601 2nd Avenue, tel: 206 448-8522), which sells merchandise from previous seasons for a fraction of the cost. The Rack offers some of the best buys in the city for everything from casual to couture.

For those on a camping tour, stop by the **Federal Army Navy Surplus Inc** (2112 1st Avenue, tel: 206 443-1818) where basics include duffle bags, camp stoves and flight gear. Then there's Gap retailer **Old Navy**, for fashionable, budget-conscious hipsters (601 Pine Street, tel: 206 264-9341).

Pike Place Market also has dozens of craft artisans who frequent the upper stalls of the main market, as well as shops in the downstairs, indoor areas. The two levels underneath the main market include shops ranging from antiquarian books, a magic store, a comic shop, fabric stores, ethnic grocery stores, incense and all sorts of other hidden treasures. Pick up a market guide at the **Read All About It** international newsstand (tel: 206 624-0140) in the kiosk just next to the market's icon, *Rachel the Pig*, and browse your home-town paper, too.

Downtown, Reasonable

Many people interested in shopping will go on some version of this downtown retail cruise. They'll start at **Pacific Place Mall** (600 Pine Street; wwwpacificplace.com), which includes national chains **Pottery Barn**, **J Crew**, **Aveda** and the **Body Shop**, then head next door to the Seattle-based **Nordstrom** department store at Fifth and Pine (tel: 206 628-2111).

Besides the best window displays, Nordstrom also has the city's most comprehensive cosmetics and perfume counters. If you have trouble finding that special gift, go to the Nordstrom concierge, and discover how they earned their (now nationwide) reputation for impeccable service. At the center of the shopping district is **Westlake Center** (400 Pine Street), which specializes in mid-level chains like **Foot Locker**, **Talbots** and **Trade Secret**.

Other shopping must-visits include: the department store **Bon-Macy's** (300 Pine Street, tel: 206 506-6671), **The Gap** (5th Avenue and Pine Street, tel: 206 254-8000) and **Banana Republic** (500 Pike Street, tel: 206 622-2303), housed in the lovingly preserved Coliseum Theatre, a reminder of the glory days of the city.

Finally, for one-of-a-kind deals on second-hand fashions, check out **Alexandra's** (412

left: café society
right: buy food fresh from the market

Olive Way, tel: 206 623-1214) a designer and consignment store, and **Rudy's Vintage** (109 Pine Street, tel: 206 682-6586).

Downtown, Expensive

Here are recommendations for those seeking high quality and guaranteed originality. **Alhambra** (101 Pine Street, tel: 206 621-9571) offers fashionable women's clothing and furnishings, and is known for its piano recitals as well as its live models on the first Thursday of each month.

If art and architecture books are your thing, visit **Peter Miller** (1930 1st Avenue, tel: 206 441-4114) for those sumptuous coffee-table books that will have you investing in a new coffee table just to hold them. Next door is Seattle's original high-fashion boutique, **Baby and Co** (1936 1st Avenue, tel: 206 448-4077).

Cross the street to **Isadora's Antique Clothing** (1915 1st Avenue, tel: 206 441-7711), Seattle's premiere vintage clothing source. If you're expecting the paparazzi, visit **Mario's** (1513 6th Avenue, tel: 206 223-1461) for a tailored suit and other extravagances. **Ped** (1115 1st Avenue, tel: 206 292-1767) has the best selection of shoes in town. Then there's **Cicada** (1121 1st Avenue, tel: 206 652-2434), a locally-owned salon featuring handmade bridal design and evening wear for women and men.

Barney's New York (1420 5th Avenue, tel: 206 622-6300) is where many of Seattle's celebrities can be spotted 'spending it' on things like mohair T-shirts, cashmere su and matching shoes. Other top-drawer h spots include the boutiques in and around **Rainier Tower**, the **Fairmont Olympic Ho** and also the **5th Avenue Theatre**. Final for custom-made jewelry as well as origir sculpture, check out **Twist** (600 Pine Stre tel: 206 315-8080), offering all-America crafted pieces with an emphasis on silver a precious gemstones.

Capitol Hill

Furniture, art, vintage clothing and book sho are springing up here, mostly along Pike a Pine streets (known locally as 'the Pike-Pi Corridor') and along Broadway. Many of t shops are in the inexpensive-to-modera range, though expensive places are includ and noted.

Up the Pike-Pine Corridor you'll find stor filled with lots of one-off treasures, inclu ing **Le Frock** (317 E Pine Street, tel: 206 62 5339), featuring second-hand and vinta clothing for men and women, and **Edie's** (3 E Pine, tel: 206 839-1111), which has t hippest footwear anywhere in the city.

Contemporary furniture and fixture c lectors will enjoy **Area 51** (401 E Pine Stre tel: 206 568-4782). **Fallout Records, Boo and Comics** (1506 E Olive Way, tel: 206 32 2662) was a major force during the glory da of grunge music.

Lipstick Traces (500 E Pine Street, t 206 329-2813) is a sweet salon where t stylish owner features carefully crafted co collections, like Queen Bee bags and acce sories, and hand-decorated notebooks.

Toys in Babeland (707 E Pike, tel: 2 328-2914) is easily the most customer-friend erotica and sex shop in the Northwest. I just a few doors from **Martin-Zambito Fi Arts** (721 E Pike Street, 206 726-9509), quiet gallery for 19th to 21st-century Nort west and regional art with an emphasis women artists.

On Broadway, the independently owne **Bailey/Coy Books** (414 Broadway Avenue tel: 206 323-8842) has a knowledgeable sta a wide range of titles and a good selection gay and lesbian literature. Also on this stre **Metro Clothing Co.** (231 Broadway Aven E, tel: 206 726-7978) has a costume-wort collection of vinyl, patent leather, platfor

Left: Fallout Records

oes and Goth get-ups. Finally, alternative
usic lovers will want to visit **Orpheum** (618
oadway Avenue E, tel: 206 322-6370), a
cord and CD store where independent, hip-
p and rock co-exist in relative harmony, if
t exactly peace.

emont

attle's funky-neighborhood-on-the-way-up
ll has great idiosyncratic stores and is a fine
ace to shop when you've got a few extra
ins jingling in your pocket. Fremont's var-
d shops include **Burnt Sugar** (601 N 35th
reet, tel: 206 545-0699) selling vintage and
ntemporary jewelry, furniture and house-
ld accessories.

Deluxe Junk (3518 Fremont Place N, tel:
6 634-2733) has fascinating things (furni-
re, knick-knacks, jewelry) in a surprisingly
all space. Like grandfather's attic but with
ss dust – and with price tags, of course.

Eyes on Fremont (4254 Fremont N, tel:
6 634-3375), sells high quality and stylish
ecs for a lot (and we're talking, *a lot*) less
an its competitors. **Fremont Place Book
ompany** (621 N 35th Street, tel: 206 547-
70) is an independent bookstore with a won-
rful view of the heart of Fremont. Browse
d people-watch in one place.

Fans of clothes from the 1950s through the
70s will discover a paradise packed with

vintage clothing at **Fritzi Ritz** (750 N 34th
Street, tel: 206 633-0929). Fun treasures like
bowling shirts and funky ball gowns are just
some of the items on sale. You'll find similar goods and more at the **Fremont Antique
Mall** (3419 Fremont Place N, tel: 206 548-
9140), which has a variety of stalls manned by
independent vendors.

Les Amis (3420 Evanston Avenue N, tel:
206 632-2877) is an elegant, original clothing boutique that features fresh-milled soap
and fun jewelry along with scarves, frocks
and sleek and sensual lingerie. Well-designed
Sonic Boom (3414 Fremont Avenue N, tel:
206 547-2666) is a friendly independent music
store, popular with local musicians.

South Lake Union

Finally, out on its own in the South Lake Union
neighborhood (a 15-minute walk down from
Capitol Hill or a ten-minute jaunt from downtown Seattle) is **REI** (222 Yale Avenue N, tel:
206 223-1944 www.rei.com). This local business was one of the first to make outdoor clothing so stylish that they became fashionable
indoors. Now REI is known around the nation.

Selling alongside the clothes is good-qual-
ity equipment for camping, fishing, hiking
and climbing. There are even indoor 'trails'
where you can find out how those boots grip,
and a spiffy climbing rock.

ove: Seattleites are great lovers of books; the weather probably helps

EATING OUT

As recently as the early 1980s, fine dining in Seattle meant steak and seafood, which was as likely to come from Maine as fresh from the market. But then Seattle chefs like Le Gourmand's Bruce Naftalay developed a style of cooking based on French techniques and flair but using local ingredients. This became known as 'Northwest cuisine.' The region is blessed with excellent seafood, vegetables, herbs and spices, so finding the right tastes to blend was easy.

Fusion, an offshoot of Northwest cuisine, came to prominence in the early 1990s, around the same time as American politicians and investors began to say 'Pacific Rim,' referring to common values of the West Coast, Alaskan and Asian peoples. Early experiments mixed a little Asian with a little French, then cautiously added other influences. Recently, fusion has pulled back from the more bizarre excesses and is content to put an exotic flourish or two on local dishes. Seattle also has excellent Italian and ethnic restaurants, some of which are included on this list.

$ = $5–$25 for entrees
$$ = $20–$40 for entrees
$$$ = $40 up, sometimes way up

Brasa
2107 3rd Avenue
Tel: 206 728-4220; www.brasa.com
During the dot.com boom, Belltown was flooded with expensive, stylish eateries with wooden interiors, moodily lit bars, and wait staff who appeared to be moonlighting from fashion shoots. Only a few years later, many of these had disappeared. This restaurant is a worthy survivor. Signature dishes are duck confit and beef tenderloin. There is also a varied bar menu including rabbit and shrimp paella and a cheeringly crisp grape pizza. $

Café Flora
2901 E Madison Street
Tel: 206 325-9100; www.cafeflora.com
This vegetarian restaurant has unexpected pleasures both on the menu and in the seating (if you can, sit in the conservatory-like area with its small fountain). The soups and salads are consistently good, but main meals can be stodgy or bizarre (though the Portobello mushroom Wellington is neither, just flaky, original and delicious). $$

Café Lago
2305 24th Avenue E
Tel: 206 329-8005
This Italian restaurant has a mantelpiece of awards for its wood-fired pizza, though our favorite is the lasagna, in thin layers as delicate as pastry. The atmosphere is not especially romantic, unless exquisite food sets your heart pounding. $$

Café Septieme
214 Broadway Avenue E
Tel: 206 860-8858
This Broadway bistro is the coolest eatery on Capitol Hill for its people-watching, inexpensive but inventive menu, strong drinks and, particularly, the staff, who range from charming to coldly indifferent. It's darkly lit, with blood-red walls, deep booths and a fine dessert selection. $–$$

Café Campagne
1600 Post Alley
Tel: 206 728-2233
www.campagnerestaurant.com

The 'little brother' of Campagne restaurant is in no way inferior to its expensive sibling, just less complicated. Entrees are a la carte, for example, and you can walk in wearing your work clothes without feeling underdressed. French Provencal is the style, and the results, particularly the coffee-and-pastry breakfast and the lunch patés, are glorious. $$

Campagne
Inn at the Market
86 Pike Street
Tel: 206 728-2800
www.campagnerestaurant.com
Campagne does the right things right. The service is impeccable, the appetizers – especially the soups – are exquisite, and the wine list is comprehensive without being overwhelming. A wine steward friend confides that their red and white burgundy list is the best in the city. The specialty is French, but of the approachable sort. Anyone who appreciates food will appreciate Campagne. $$$

Canlis
2576 Aurora Avenue N
Tel: 206 283-3313; www.canlis.com
In business since 1950 (an eternity in restaurant years), Canlis has not rested on its laurels, and has shifted the menu toward the Asian influences now *de rigueur*. It also has a terrific wine list, so make time to check it out thoroughly. A hint for vegetarians: try the immaculately prepared and varied bento box. For everyone else: do not miss the steak. $$$

Cascadia Restaurant
328 1st Avenue
Tel: 206 448-8884
www.cascadiarestaurant.com
Chef Kerry Sear uses the best and freshest ingredients of the Cascade region: smoked salmon, wild mushrooms and halibut, for example. Sear is a vegetarian, but you'd never know it from his masterful preparations of venison, lamb and turkey. Your best bet is to choose one of the three seven-course tasting menus. Expensive, but worth it. $$-$$$

Coastal Kitchen
429 15th Avenue E
Tel: 206 322-1145; www.chowfoods.com
This hip Capitol Hill hang-out keeps diners

guessing with its changing menu. How the cooks do so well at so many different ethnic styles is a mystery, but they do. There's never any doubt, though, about their weekend brunches, especially the pork-chop plate. $

Crave
1621 12th Avenue
Tel: 206 388-0526; www.cravefood.com
Crave bills itself as serving 'honest food' and its menu and friendly service live up to the billing. Food changes by the season, but might include curried lamb, goat cheese gnocchi and shiitake mac and cheese. $

The Dahlia Lounge
2001 4th Avenue
Tel: 206 682-4142; www.tomdouglas.com
Restaurateur Tom Douglas got his start with this elegant place before opening Etta's Seafood, the Palace Kitchen and Lola. The menu has an Asian influence in the seafood preparation. Dungeness crab cakes are moist, well-seasoned, and a highlight, but if it's decadent fulfillment you're after, hold back: donuts are made on-site, and arrive with jam and vanilla mascarpone on the side. $$

Etta's Seafood
2020 Western Avenue
Tel: 206 443-6000; www.tomdouglas.com
It's not all seafood at Etta's (there's delectable chicken and polenta), but fish is the highlight. Don't skimp on the side dishes, either; the servers give excellent advice on what best complements what. $$

night of the week, serving plate after plate of ultra-fresh seafood: crispy calamari, grilled scallops, Thai crab cakes, fried razor clams, wok-blackened ahi tuna, and more. To encourage sharing, platters of seafood – whole fried rockfish, mussels, Dungeness crab, grilled Gulf shrimp – are offered by the pound. In summer, the front windows open up to the street and the sun setting over Puget Sound. $$

Galerias
611 Broadway Avenue E
Tel: 206 322-5757
This Mexican restaurant has a singularly ornate style that goes beyond its carved wooden screens and vast metal menus. Every dish, including the amazing *camarones al ajilo* (shrimp and button mushrooms drenched in garlic butter) and the supreme *enchiladas con mole* are works of art, as are the huge margaritas. Delicious, remarkably affordable, and Galerias has even got seating right on people-watching Broadway. $–$$

Eva Restaurant and Wine Bar
2227 N 56th Street
Tel: 206 633-3538
This noisy bistro near Green Lake offers a seasonally changing menu and a thoughtful wine list. Desserts are standouts. $$

5 Spot
1502 Queen Anne Avenue N
Tel: 206 285-7768; www.chowfoods.com
Like other restaurants owned by Peter Levy and Jeremy Hardy, the 5 Spot has a menu that travels from Texas to New England and beyond. Though all three meals are served, breakfast is the most popular at this top-of-Queen-Anne-Hill institution. Try fried green tomatoes (in season), honey-stung chicken or 'Brother John's all-day breakfast.' $

Five Point
415 Cedar Street
Tel: 206 441-4777
A local legend, the Five Point has been serving cheap, tasty diner food since 1928. It really comes to life after the bars close at 2 am. $

Flying Fish
2234 1st Avenue
Tel: 206 728-8595;
www.flyingfishseattle.com
This Belltown favorite is lively almost every

El Gaucho
2505 1st Avenue
Tel: 206 728-1337
The movie set you just wandered onto is one of the gorgeous speakeasies from the 1930s, where diners at elevated tables ate fabulous food, flirted across the room, and enjoyed an elaborate floor show. No floor show now, but everything else is here from the steaks (try the ostrich or delicate tuna steaks as a change of pace) to the expensive bar and cigar room. If the food wasn't so good you might feel it was a bit hokey, but go on, give in to the fantasy. $$$

Harvest Vine
2701 E Madison
Tel: 206 320-9771
This small restaurant is dominated by a tapas bar, where customers gather for outstanding Basque cooking. Particularly recommended are the seafood dishes, including the calamari as well as the spicy chorizo sausage. $$

House of Hong
409 8th Avenue S
Tel: 206 622-7997
This International District restaurant is where those in the know go for *dim sum*, the morning

Above: eat so near the water that fish practically swim onto your plate

ing and mid-day meal of delicious steamed appetizers brought to your table. Go with big appetites and with a large group if you can manage it, and aim for between 11am and 3pm to get the best variety. $

Kingfish Café
602 19th Avenue E
Tel: 206 320-8757
Southern soul food done up with style, sauce and smiles. The grits go well with everything and the catfish is pretty miraculous. Long lines attest to the café's popularity, particularly for weekend brunch. $$

Lark
926 12th Avenue
Tel: 206 323-5275; www.larkseattle.com
Sharable plates, an oft-changing menu and knowledgeable servers add to the appeal at this charming Capitol Hill bistro. Flickering candlelight and the buzz of the food-savvy crowd of beautiful people (and there *is* a crowd) complement dishes that range from seared Sonoma foie gras to carpaccio of yellowtail. Vegetables might be wild mushrooms with garlic, olive oil and sea salt. Desserts like Valrhona chocolate hazelnut tart or frozen lemon parfait with lemon verbena jus are worth waiting for. $$

Le Gourmand
825 NW Market Street
Tel: 206 784-3463
Bruce Natalay, the godfather of Northwest cuisine, gets to show off his skill at Le Gourmand. Using fresh seasonal vegetables, day-of-sale seafood and herbs from his own garden, the three-course menu with an a la carte dessert selection is temptation at its most persuasive. Be sure to book in advance; it's worth every penny. $$$

Le Pichet
1933 1st Avenue
Tel: 206 256-1499
As pleasing for its high ceilings and marble floors as for the delicately prepared food, this is a grand place for romantics to sample the good life. The first-rate entrees are complemented by a fine selection of cheeses and pâtés. The wine selection is good and reasonably priced. $$

Market Street Grill
1744 NW Market Street
Tel: 206 789-6766
Although Ballard is becoming a happening neighborhood for artists, musicians and other bohemians, it's still surprising to find such an exceptional restaurant as the Market Street. The Myer's lemon chicken and the lamb are highlights of the menu, and the service is truly spectacular, possibly due to the owners both having in the past managed some of Seattle's best restaurants. A delightful treat in an unexpected neighborhood. $$–$$$

Metropolitan Grill
820 2nd Avenue
Tel: 206 624-3287
www.themetropolitangrill.com
With the number of awards the Metropolitan has received as 'Seattle's Best Steakhouse,' you might expect complacency. Not a bit of it. The steaks are done within a degree of your preferred temperature and break the scales with their girth, but it's the service with a flourish from the elegant wait staff that really makes this place. $$$

Palace Kitchen
2030 5th Avenue
Tel: 206 448-2001
This 5th Avenue restaurant is consistent in terms of overall quality of the menu, but it's the appetizers that really set the place on the map. They're great value and surprisingly generous. The kitchen is open till 1am, and the place can get pretty boisterous later in the evening. $$–$$$

Palisade
Elliot Bay Marina
2601 W Marina Place

Right: a Northwest cuisine theme

Tel: 206 285-1000
www.palisaderestaurant.com
The flagship of the local Restaurants Unlimited line (which includes Cutters and Palomino), this restaurant is a little out of the way, but worth the trip. The setting is unique, featuring a sliver of saltwater stocked with fish, right in the main room and a view of the Olympic Mountains through huge windows that would be worth the price of dinner even if the food wasn't excellent. Several grills and ovens offer a variety of food styles, and the staff are experienced in producing a sense of occasion. $$$

Red Mill Burgers

312 N 67th Street
Tel: 206 783-6382; www.redmillburgers.com
In the eternal debate over who has the best hamburgers in Seattle, Red Mill always makes the top five, but there's no argument at all about who does the best onion rings. This venerable Seattle restaurant has been doing things its own way for generations, and still people flock here. A second branch is located in Interbay at 1613 W Dravus Street (tel: 206 284-6363). $

Saigon Bistro

1032 S Jackson #202
Tel: 206 329-4939
Located above the Viet Wah Asian market, this place is a little bit light on ambiance, but the wonderful, well-prepared food more than makes up for the plain-jane decor. Try the duck and cabbage soup, or the tapioca-like bean drink. Best of all, it's one of the cheapest dinner menus in the International District. $

Stumbling Goat

6722 Greenwood Avenue N.
Tel: 206 784-3535
A Phinney Ridge restaurant that offers a particularly good range of seafood and seasonal vegetables and herbs, though the Goat's par roasted chicken is also a stand-out. A nic alternative to the meat and fish on the men is their great vegetarian risotto, which man ages to be ideally *al dente* while being luxu riantly creamy. $$

Tulio

1100 5th Avenue
Tel: 206 624-5500; www.tulio.com
Located in the Hotel Vintage Park, Tulio far more just than a hotel restaurant. Th authentic Italian menu includes house-cure meats, pastas and baked foccacia. Start wit sweet potato gnocchi with sage butter and mas carpone, advance to chanterelle mushroo risotto and feast on grilled herb lamb sirloi Save room for gelato. $$

Union

1400 1st Avenue
Tel: 206 833-8000; www.unionseattle.com
Small portions of exquisite food are the dra at this large downtown restaurant. From Dungeness crab salad with avocado and basi to grilled squab with mushrooms and age balsamic vinegar, to Muscovy duck breast wit baked figs in a port reduction, everything perfectly matched. Five- and seven-cours tasting menus are also available, with a lighte early-evening menu served in the bar. $$$

Via Tribunali

913 E Pike Street
Tel: 206 322-9234
Be prepared to wait for a table at this dark sexy and crowded Capitol Hill hot-spot. Mos of the ingredients are imported from Italy, an the Neapolitan-style pizzas are broiled in fire-stoked oven. $

Wild Ginger Asian Restaurant

1401 3rd Avenue
Tel: 206 623-4450
Although dishes hail from Singapore Bangkok, Saigon and Djakarta, this extreme popular Asian restaurant doesn't suffer fro a lack of focus. Favorites include the coconu brothed laksa (a Malaysian seafood soup) an the fragrant duck. The mahogany satay ba offers a range of skewers, among them sca lops, eggplant, wild boar, lemongrass chicke and fish – all of them are good. $$

Left: Asian delicacies

NIGHTLIFE

...ve music of every kind, dancing, theater, ...adings, the symphony, the ballet, the opera, ...lleries, movies: it's a packed schedule for ...ght owls in Seattle. Specific events and ...tails can be found in the listings sections ...free weeklies (*Seattle Weekly* and *The ...ranger*), as well as in the 'What's Happen...g' sections, published every Thursday, in ...e daily newspapers.

...e Arts

...addition to theatre *(see page 57)*, Seattleites ...joy a top-drawer classical music scene. The **...attle Symphony** (tel: 206 215-4747; ...ww.seattlesymphony.org), under the direc...n of conductor Gerard Schwartz, has pro...ced an impressive canon, primarily from ...merican tonalists, Schwartz's favorite com...sers. In their splendid home at Benaroya ...all, the players have sumptuous surround...gs and fine acoustics.

   The Seattle Opera (tel: 206 389-7676; ...ww.seattleopera.org) has a year-round sea...n, but have made their reputation by tack...g Wagner's Ring Cycle every four years, ...th critically-acclaimed results. In 2003, the ...mpany moved into its new state-of-the-art ...me, Marion Oliver McCaw Hall, on the ...attle Center grounds.

   Seattle's classical dance scene is smaller ...an its vibrant theatre or music scenes, but the ...cific **Northwest Ballet** (tel: 206 441-2424;

www.pnb.org) is a well-respected regional dance company where the annual, very popular, production of *The Nutcracker* features a cheerily peculiar design by the children's book illustrator Maurice Sendak of *Where the Wild Things Are* fame.

Live Music/Dancing

Live music is increasingly rare, as clubs hire DJs instead of live musicians for economy, and in response to those raised on hip-hop, house and electronic. Yet even in the glory days of grunge, the Seattle club crowd had a trademark reaction to live musicians, which

...bove: jazz in a Pioneer Square club
...ight: go dancing in the Pampas Room

was: stand around, sway slightly, and look
unimpressed. (You can still see this oddity
most nights at the Crocodile.) So if your
favorite band happens to be playing while
you're here, by all means go. But don't think
that a quiet audience with seemingly bored
faces means the band are doing a bad job; those
silent spectators are just showing apprecia-
tion of the music in an 'inner sense.' It's very
Seattle; join in.

The Crocodile Cafe
2200 2nd Avenue SE
Tel: 206 441-5611
The past and the present of Seattle's music
scene are one and the same at the venerable
Crocodile, where grunge had its home and
whatever is going to come next will probably debut. Live music throughout the week,
and tasty café food as well. No dancing, just
swaying back and forth.

Graceland
109 Eastlake Avenue E
Tel: 206 381-3094
This used to be the Off-Ramp, scene of many
a Seattle rock triumph, and they still offer a fun
if variable collection of live acts.

Last Supper Club
124 S Washington Street
Tel: 206 748-9975
A nice bar menu and a few tables becor
crowded and potentially unpleasant after 10p
when the music on this two-floor dance cl
kicks in. Like all Pioneer Square venues, st
away over the weekend unless you're fo
of booze-soaked fraternity boys and high
rowdy times.

Neighbours
1509 Broadway
Tel: 206 324-5358
www.neighboursnightclub.com
The grand-uncle of Seattle's gay club sce
has a big bar, bigger dance floor, and balcon
for sipping drinks and checking out the flo
below. The only thing that's changed, desp
cosmetic facelifts, is that it's not so gay an
more; some nights, the clientele is 50 perce
straight. Friendly and trouble-free atmosphe

The Re-bar
1114 Howell Street
Tel: 206 233-9873
The signs on the door say it all: if you'
homophobic, racist, or uptight in any sort
way, don't go in. The Re-bar caters to a mul
ethnic, multi-sexual preference crowd wi
music from disco through hip-hop, taking
every permutation of the last 30 years. A gre
place to dance, so take folks who like to mov

The Showbox
1426 1st Avenue
Tel: 206 628-3151
Seattle's premiere mid-sized venue is classi
inside than you'd guess from its garish ma
quee, a hangover from its days as a come
club. Now the space features touring ban
and dance nights. Crowded and a bit tatter
most nights (except for the elegant loung
the Green Room), but with the right crov
and the right vibe, this venue can't be beat.

The Vogue
1516 11th Avenue
Tel: 206 324-5778
The premiere music hang-out for the altern
tive crowd, the Vogue's Goth and fetish nigh
draw the black-leather-and-chains folks. Oth
evenings, there's disco, techno and the like

Above: Neighbours has balconies, a big bar and an even bigger dance floor

ars and Wine Bars

rinking age in the US is 21 for all alcohol, cluding beer and wine. Stringent liquor laws Washington mean it's likely you will be ked to provide valid ID at many of the bars d clubs listed here. Seattle's own convo- ted liquor laws mean that some places you'd pect to get a full bar you'll only find beer d wine, while other spots are barely big ough to contain the full bar they're licensed have.

A law passed in late 2005 dictates that all rs (and restaurants) in Seattle are smoke- ee. At press time, club owners were pre- cting that banning cigarettes would be bad r business. Stay tuned.)

Entertainment after 2 am: contrary to offi- al reports, there *is* after-hours entertainment Seattle, at least on the weekends. Most of ese places don't serve booze (and those that so are strictly under the bar), but they do fer dancing and a place to hang till dawn. he best way to track them down is to ask ound just before closing time, particularly if u're near the Pioneer Square or Belltown eas. Be discreet, and don't be disappointed you strike out.

libi Room
Pike Street
l: 206 623-3180
dden in a cobbled section of Post Alley near e Pike Place Market, the Alibi Room has oved from its original niche, as the hang-out r Seattle's film scene, because that scene's oved farther up the coast to Vancouver. A rary of screenplays attest to its past life, t these days the place does better with a lect but reasonable menu of soups, salads d sandwiches, a long but crowded bar, and casional live music or DJ in the downstairs om. A snazzy place for a rendezvous or to unite with friends.

d Juju Lounge
25 10th Avenue
l: 206 709-9951
echno Goth' is the theme of the Bad Juju. ld creations hang from the walls and voodoo t blends with glasswork and iron fixtures. e young and varied clientele bring their own cabulary to the place, which varies nightly cording to the crowd.

Capitol Club
414 E Pine Street
Tel: 206 325-2149
Don't misunderstand: the downstairs restau- rant in the Capitol Club is very nice; Mediter- ranean food with a nice line in appetizers. But it's the upstairs lounge with its cushioned benches and outdoor balcony, and stunning wait staff (both men and women) who invari- ably will flirt you into another drink, that pulls in the regulars.

The Comet
922 E Pike Street
Tel: 206 323-9853
For a taste of what Seattle was like before the crowds and the dot.con hype and hyperbole, this exuberantly low-down-and-dirty estab- lishment is the place to go. Noisy and with walls covered by years of graffiti, the spirit of grunge is the reigning on-site specter. The beer is cheap.

Nite Lite Lounge
1926 Second Avenue
Tel: 206 443-0899
Country music on the jukebox, old and wise bar staff, a back area featuring set pieces from a movie shot years ago: disparate elements that come together in a place that's too proud to be a dive. Strong drinks in a pleasing place.

Pampas Room
90 Wall Street
Tel: 206 728-1337; www.elgaucho.com
Located beneath the swanky El Gaucho, the Pampas is a ritzy dream of an old-fashioned good time. A small stage often features live music, the food is snazzy, the bartenders serve grand drinks, and the atmosphere is the 1940s all over again. A nice older crowd enjoying a bygone era.

The Triangle Lounge
3507 Fremont Place N
Tel: 206 632-0880
Where the young, the beautiful, or just the brash go on Fremont weekends, and where the defiant inhabitants of older Fremont (hip- pies, hepsters, and those nostalgic for both) come during the day and during the week. Live music some nights, and a tasty bar menu for those hungry moments.

CALENDAR OF EVENTS

January

New Year's Eve includes fireworks from the Space Needle, in addition to music-filled parties and celebrations in many of the city's bars and restaurants.

Chinese New Year is celebrated in the International District with parades, food, fireworks and special events. Tel: 206 382-1197; www.cidbia.org.

February

The *Northwest Flower and Garden Show* is held over President's Day weekend. Gardeners swarm over 300 booths in the downtown Convention Center. Tel: 206 789-5333; www.gardenshownw.com.

March

St Patrick's Day Parade. On March 17th, a small but enthusiastic band of Irish-Americans parade from City Hall to Westlake Center, with bagpipers, dancers, bands and Celtic entertainment. A fun run, lots of bar activity and beer dyed green; www.irishclub.org.

Whirligig at Seattle Center is a carnival for kids throughout the month with rides and free entertainment. Tel: 206 684-7200.

April

The *Cherry Blossom & Japanese Cultural Festival* is a spring traditionally-themed and delicate festival held at the Seattle Center. Te 206 684-7200.

Taste Washington is a one-day event celebrating the state's foods and wines with educational seminars, live jazz and hundreds award-winning Washington wines. Tel: 2(667-9463, www.tastewashington.org

May

The *Northwest Folklife Festival*, one of t biggest gatherings of folk musicians in t country, takes place over Memorial Day wee end at the Seattle Center. Musicians and craft people from around the world come her Grills flame with ethnic foods. Beware dru circles and patchouli overdose, but by a means experience the scene. Tel: 206 68 7300, www.nwfolklife.org.

The *Opening Day of Yachting Season* is pleasantly democratic event that belies i snooty title. On the first Saturday of May, cre races and a parade of boats from the humb to the grand join a regatta leading from La Union to Lake Washington.

The *Seattle International Film Festival* is o of America's least publicized and most we regarded, with an emphasis on independe work and films from other countries. Holl wood blockbusters are in short supply, b fans certainly aren't, standing in lengthy lin seeking celluloid nirvana. Mid-May to mi June. Tel: 206 324-9996; www.seattlefilm.or Perhaps the most impressive local gatherir

Above: Seattle celebrates Chinese New Year and the Japanese Cultural Festival

of theatre, dance and music all year is the *Seattle International Children's Festival*, held at Seattle Center in mid-May, featuring Chinese acrobats, whirling dervishes, Ukranian clowns and other acts. Tel: 206 684-7338.

June

The *Pike Place Market Street Festival* has free entertainment and special events celebrating the soul of Seattle's life. Tel: 206 587-0351; www.seattleinternational.org.

The *Fremont Fair*, on the third weekend in June, is timed roughly to the summer solstice. It's a defiant reminder of the neighborhood's funkiness *(see page 40)*. Tel: 206 694-6706, www.freemontfair.org

July

The *Fourth of July-Ivar Festival* at the waterfront has food, a fishing derby, and one of the three major fireworks displays put on around the city. Also on the July 4th weekend, the Center for Wooden Boats hosts the Lake Union Wooden Boat Festival, with rides and other maritime activites. 1010 Valley Street, tel: 206 382-2628; www.cwb.org

Seafair runs from late July to early August – a vast civic celebration with a torchlight parade, hydroplane boat races, stunt jets from the US Navy's Blue Angels, sporting events, and open houses on docked Navy vessels. For our money, one of the best events is the fabled milk-carton derby races at Green Lake. Tel: 206 728-0123; www.seafair.com.

Bite of Seattle is a food festival at Seattle Center. Over 60 local restaurants participate, offering samples from their menus. Tel: 245 283-5050; www.biteofseattle.com.

August

Billed as the world's largest marijuana-reform rally, *Seattle Hempfest* takes over Myrtle Edwards Park for a weekend every August. Tel: 206 781-5734, www.hempfest.org

September

Bumbershoot is a massive arts festival held at Seattle Center over the Labor Day weekend, featuring rock headliners, theatre, dance, music, literary events and an art gallery. The music in particular draws huge crowds; there's a general admission fee per day, or you can buy multi-day passes; www.bumbershoot.org.

Right: Halloween house in Ballard

The *Puyallup Fair* is 35 miles (55km) out of town, but this old-fashioned state fair draws many Seattleites on an annual pilgrimage to see prize livestock, enter bake-offs, and go on wacky carnival rides. Takes place over 17 days. Tel: (253) 841-5045; www.thefair.com.

October

Halloween, October 31st, is an increasingly adult holiday in the US, and now all the real raucousness kicks off in the evening. Capitol Hill and Fremont get especially wild and fun, with revelers in costumes vying to show the most skin while preserving anonymity.

November

Winterfest includes ice skating, music and more ; late November through December. Tel: 206 684-7200; www.seattlecenter.com.

On the Friday after Thanksgiving, 3,000 runners participate in the *Seattle Marathon* (and another 5,000 run the Half Marathon). Tel: 206 729-3660; www.seattlemarathon.org.

December

Glowing luminaria are lit along the 2.8-mile trail circling Green Lake during the *Pathway of Lights*. Second Saturday in December, 5.30 – 8.30pm. Tel: 206 684-0780.

Christmas Ships is a parade of illuminated boats that sails in lakes Washington and Union throughout the month. Tel: 206 623-1445.

Christmas shows include productions of *A Christmas Carol* (the most celebrated at ACT) and other Yuletide fare. Pacific Northwest Ballet presents *The Nutcracker*, with sets by children's illustrator Maurice Sendak.

Science Center

Amphitheatre

Children's Theatre

Children's Museum

KeyArena

Theatres

Fun Forest

Space Needle

Center House

Monorail

Exp. Music P.

Memorial S

Practical Information

GETTING THERE

By Air

Seattle-Tacoma International Airport, or Sea-Tac as it is more commonly known, is an international airport served by most major national and international airlines. It is located 13 miles (21km) from Seattle but is easily accessible by regular bus, taxi and shuttle services. For details on the airport go online (www.portseattle.org/seatac/) or call the information line; tel: 206 431-4444 or (800) 544-1965.

By Rail

Amtrak (www.amtrak.com), the national rail line, serves Seattle at the Union Station at 3rd and Jackson, or at the King Street Station a block away. Tel: 800-USA-RAIL. Trains are infrequent, but connections from the East include the *Empire Builder* from Chicago, the *California Zephyr* from Denver, and from the south, the *Coast Starlight*. This last route, which travels south through Tacoma, Olympia, Vancouver (Washington) and Portland, Oregon, takes a scenic route along the coast. There is also the *Cascades* line running up to Vancouver in Canada, but fair warning: some of the 'rail' connections offered by Amtrak are actually bus lines, which you can find out about online.

By Road

Seattle is served by two major freeways, Interstate 5 (better known as I-5) which runs from Canada all the way through America down to the Mexican border, and Interstate 90 (I-90) which heads east towards Chicago and Boston. Despite heavy congestion in the immediate area, Federal and state highways tend to be well-maintained with frequent signs, rest stops and service stations.

By Sea

Seattle is linked to the islands nearby through the efficient Washington State Ferry Sys-tem, with a regular ferry service to Vancouver and Victoria in British Columbia, Canada. Private cruise ship lines also visit Seattle, though the Alaska State Ferry System, which at one time docked in Seattle, now terminates up the coast at Bellingham, Washington.

Travel Essentials

Clothing

As befits the weather, for decades the Seattle fashion has been casual, with a predominance of jeans and flannel shirts. REI and Eddie Bauer, both homegrown stores, perfected their rugged-yet-stylish look here. Some businesses have started a move toward more formal dress but the coat-and-tie look is more likely to be seen in restaurants than in offices.

Customs

US Customs allows anyone over 21 to bring one bottle of liquor and 200 cigarettes duty free into the country. All gifts must be declared. Any gifts worth from $400 to $1,000 incur a 10 percent charge. Gifts over $1,000 are charged a 'duty right' that varies according to the item.

Electricity

In the US and Canada the voltage is 110v, and the plugs have either two (flat) or three (two flat and one round) prongs. Three-prong plugs don't fit into two-slotted sockets, but adapters to convert one voltage to another are easy to come by.

Time Zones

Seattle is in the Pacific

Left: Seattle Center sign
Right: bus stop

Time Zone, the same as California and Oregon, 3 hours behind the East Coast and 8 hours behind London. Daylight Savings Time means that on the first Sunday in April clocks move forward one hour, and on the last Sunday in October they go back one hour. In 2007, these days will change to the second Sunday in March and the first Sunday in November.

Visas and Passports

Some visitors to the US are required to have a visa. Exceptions are participants in the Visa Waiver Pilot Program (including citizens of the UK and many European countries), plus Canadians and Mexicans with valid border passes. Non-American *and* American citizens should note that if they take one of the many excursions from Seattle into Canada, border control will ask for identity papers; a valid passport is best.

Weather

Yes, it is often raining in Seattle. But it doesn't rain a lot. Rainfall in the Emerald City averages around 38in (96cm) a year, less than Boston, Atlanta or even New York City. But those inches fall in light rains, and the skies above Seattle are often partly cloudy, with an average of only 55 days a year of clear skies. But if you visit between April and October, you might not even see rain, as most rainfall is in winter and early spring. If you do get caught in a downpour, it'll most probably be

Above: rain or shine, fans flock to Safeco Park

mild in temperature. Thanks to warm oceanic currents, the temperature rarely dips below freezing point, while even the hottest days in the summer months tend to be pleasant and are rarely humid.

When to Visit

While you'll want to pack according to the season, Seattle is worth a trip at any time of year. Summer is the peak season, and many downtown hotels are booked months in advance from May through September. If you'd like to synchronize your visit with some lively activities, check the Calendar of Events *(see page 78).*

GETTING ACQUAINTED

Geography

Seattle is the largest city in the state of Washington. The population is around 570,000 in the city and over 3 million including suburbs and the commuter districts. Greater Seattle is bounded by Puget Sound and two large natural lakes, Lake Washington to the east and Lake Union to the north. Union Bay and Portage Bay link the lakes, and the Lake Washington Ship Canal links to the Sound.

Lake Washington also marks the natural divide between Seattle and the Eastside, which includes the ever-growing towns of Kirkland, Bellevue and Renton. The meandering Duwamish River and Puget Sound separate Seattle from West Seattle.

Natural geography and successive waves of immigrants have made most Seattle neighborhoods distinctive and proud of their individuality. There are real differences in temperament, look and feel between Capitol Hill and downtown Seattle, for instance, despite their close proximity.

Population (ethnicity)

Seattle is about 70 percent white, though this balance has changed in the last 25 years and undoubtedly will continue to do so. Asian Americans comprise roughly 13 percent of the population (the fastest-growing group), followed by African Americans. Far down the list at 1 percent is a small remnant of the Duwamish people who were the original inhabitants of the land.

MONEY MATTERS

Credit Cards/Travelers Checks

Credit cards, particularly Visa and Master-Card, are widely accepted throughout the United States, and may be used at ATMs to withdraw cash. In case of loss or theft call their toll-free numbers immediately: Visa – tel: (800) 847-2911, MasterCard – tel: (800) MC-ASSIST. Travelers checks in US dollars are widely accepted, but note that banks often require identification, so be sure to take your passport along.

ATMs

Several banks have ATMs, but be aware that most charge a service fee for use of their terminals by customers withdrawing cash using a card from another bank.

Money Exchange

There are three Thomas Cook exchange booths in Sea-Tac airport, two in the main terminal and one in the south satellite.

Tipping

Tipping is encouraged for good service. The accepted rate is 15–20 percent of the bill in a restaurant, 10–15 percent for taxi drivers and hair stylists, and a dollar or so for bellhops, incidental services, or a barista (coffee server) who smiles at you (this is not as rare as it may seem in 'polite' Seattle).

GETTING AROUND

From the Airport

The best deal for getting from Sea-Tac to downtown Seattle is the Metro Transit, which leaves on the half-hour until late at night. The 194 is an express bus and takes about half an hour, while the 174 bus takes about an hour. The ride is a little crowded, but it's also a good way to visit with Seattleites before you even get into the city.

Other services include taxis from the half-dozen companies that form a rank at the airport. The Grayline Airport Express (tel: 206 624-5077) connects to most of the major downtown hotels, Shuttle Express (tel: 425 981-7000) provides door-to-door van service 24 hours a day, Quick Shuttle (tel: 800 665-2122) also connects to other nearby cities. For arrival in style, the Washington Limousine Service (tel: 206 523-8000) actually offers fairly competitive rates if you've got a few people in your party.

AROUND THE CITY

By Taxi

Taxis in Seattle are plentiful and have standardized rates, so just hop in the first one you see. For long trips, cabbies are sometimes willing to haggle, otherwise you're on the meter. Greytop/Yellow Cab (tel: 206 282-8222), Orange Cab (tel: 206 522-8800)

above: flying the flag for Chinatown
right: taxis are easy to come by

By Monorail

Local advocates continue to push for an effective light rail or monorail system, but currently the only operation, the original Monorail dating from the 1962 World's Fair, connects the Westlake Center downtown with Seattle Center. It's a fun ride but limited as a form of public transportation.

By Bus

Seattle's Metro system is excellent, and is free within the downtown business area from 6am till 7pm each evening. Travel is comfortable and the company usually civil, though a few routes have a share of odd characters (particularly those in the Downtown free zone). Bike racks are available on all Metro buses, though loading and unloading is not allowed at some Downtown stops.

There are links to other regional systems via a series of park-and-ride schemes, so it's possible to travel right across the state for a few dollars, albeit with a lot of transfers. Always ask for a transfer; they're good for up to two hours after your initial trip. On weekends, you can get an all-day pass for the cost of two single tickets. Use Metro's well designed interactive website at: www.transit.metrokc.gov to plan your trip; you can even watch the progress of your bus to your stop thanks to technology. And, amazingly, you can plan your trip with the help of a live operator over the phone: tel: 206 553-3000.

By Car

The bad news up front: traffic in Seattle is unpleasant. The city runs a close second to LA for gridlock; a series of one-way streets are harrowing to visiting drivers, as are some steep hills that rival those of San Francisco; and parking is tight to non-existent in certain sections of the city (including Capitol Hill, Fremont and Downtown).

The good news is that park-and-ride schemes are plentiful. For more good news take a look at the bus section.

Car rentals are available at Sea-Tac airport and in various locales throughout the city. These include: Alamo (tel: 800 462-5266; www.alamo.com); Avis (tel: 800 331-1212; www.avis.com); Budget (tel: 800 527-0700; www.budget.com); and Hertz (tel: 800 654-3131; www.hertz.com).

By Ferry

Vashon, Winslow, Bremerton and several other nearby communities are served by the Washington State Ferry Service, and there's

Above: transportation links are good
Left: a relic from the 1962 World's Fair

easonal water taxi serving West Seattle from
e Seattle waterfront. For more details, pick
a copy of the ferry schedules at Pier 51.
ere are regular ferry services to Victoria,
ritish Columbia in Canada from Seattle at
er 69. Call 206 464-6400 for schedules and
tails (when traveling to Canada, be sure to
ing your passport, even if you're visiting
st for the day).

y Foot

destrians always have the right-of-way. Jay-
alking is illegal, and local police occasion-
ly get very officious about giving tickets.
en if there's no police car, horse or bicy-
e in sight, it's not a bad idea to wait, and
ok both ways, before crossing.

HOURS AND HOLIDAYS

usiness Hours

ost businesses are open from 9am to 5pm
onday through Friday, with shops gener-
y open till 6pm or later, and banks generally
en till 5:30pm (and until noon on Satur-
ys). Most banks and government offices
e closed during public holidays *(see the list
low for specific days)*.

ublic Holidays

uring the following public holidays most
nks and businesses are closed:
ew Year's Day – January 1
artin Luther King's Birthday – 3rd Mon-
y in January
resident's Day – 3rd Monday in Feb
emorial Day – Last Monday in May
dependence Day – July 4
abor Day – 1st Monday in September
olumbus Day – 2nd Monday in October
eteran's Day – November 11
hanksgiving – 4th Thursday in November
hristmas – December 25

arket Days

ost neighborhoods have Saturday as their
ajor market day. This is also the busiest day
r Pike Place Market, which has much less
siness on Sundays (although for that reason,
nday can be a good day to stroll around
d enjoy the sights, smells and sounds with-
t the crowds).

ight: commuters depend on ferries

ACCOMMODATION

Price per room
$$$: $120 and over
$$: $60–$120
$: under $60

You can score significant savings on many
downtown Seattle hotels off-season through
the Seattle Super Save Package. If you're visiting during the gray days from January
through March, you can also get a discount
coupon book. Tel: (800) 535-7071, www.seat-
tlesupersaver.com.

The Ace Hotel
2423 First Avenue
Telephone: 206 448-4721; www.acehotel.com
This small hostelry is right over the Cyclops
Cafe and Lounge, one of Belltown's best-
known restaurant/ bars. Popular with 20- and
30-somethings. Charmingly uncluttered
rooms and nice atmosphere. $$

The Alexis
1007 1st Avenue
*Telephone: (888) 580-1155, 206 516-5097;
www.alexishotel.com*
Comfortable, expensive, and friendly as a
wealthy uncle, the Alexis caters to visitors
who appreciate those little extra comforts.
Continental breakfast, wireless internet access
and evening wine tastings included in the

price. The building is over 100 years old but most of the rooms are well-maintained and luxurious. Particularly recommended are the spa suites, complete with whirlpool tubs and luxury details. $$$

Andra Hotel
2000 4th Avenue
Telephone: (877) 448-8600, 206 448-8600;
www.hotelandra.com
Formerly the Claremont Hotel, this stately 1926 building has been renovated, renamed and updated in minimalist Scandinavian style. Upper floors have views of Downtown, Puget Sound and the Space Needle. Downstairs, famous local chef Tom Douglas *(see 'Restaurants')* opened his fourth restaurant, Lola, here. The Belltown location is excellent. $$$

Days Inn Town Center
2205 7th Avenue
Telephone: (800) 329-7466, 206 448-3434;
www.daysinn.com
This budget chain hotel is convenient to downtown Seattle. Clean, cheap rooms in this three-story hotel are a good alternative to the airport motels that it resembles. $

Edgewater
Pier 67, 2411 Alaska Way
Telephone: (800) 624-0670, 206 728-7000;
www.edgewaterhotel.com
Seattle's only waterfront hotel, visited by the Beatles in 1964. The Liverpudlian lads even fished from the window, a popular pastime until the hotel put a stop to it. Recent improvements have given all 234 rooms gas fireplaces, knotty pine furniture and overstuffed chairs. Make sure you get one of the rooms with a water and mountain view – moe than 100 of them do. $$$

Fairmont Olympic Hotel
411 University Street
Telephone: (800) 441-1414, 206 621-1700;
www.fairmont.com/seattle
The lobby and restaurant of Seattle's most luxurious hotel may be more famous than the rooms. Refurbished fairly recently, rooms are still small-ish, but certainly comfortable. All the old-fashioned services (shoe-shining, 24 hour room service, and the like) remain, as well as on-site fitness facilities. $$$

Hotel Max
620 Stewart Street
Telephone: (866) 833-6299, 206 728-629
www.hotelmaxseattle.com
Another historic hotel that has gotten makeover in the past decade, Hotel Max bi itself as being Seattle's most artistic hote featuring the work of both established ar emerging local artists and photographers in 163 colorful rooms and welcoming publ spaces. $$-$$$

Hotel Monaco
1101 4th Avenue
Telephone: (800) 945-2240, 206 516-509.
www.monaco-seattle.com
Luxury with a certain style and quirkines The retro look of the building is fun and ecle tic. The downstairs restaurant, Sazarac, is be for appetizers and desserts, but the bar is qui a scene. Rooms have CD players and fa machines as you might expect, but who ca resist a goldfish sent up by the staff to keep yo company? $$$

Inn at El Gaucho
2505 First Avenue
Telephone: (866) 354-2824, 206 728-113.
www.inn.elgaucho.com
Located above Seattle's ultra-hip El Gauch steakhouse in Belltown, this small luxury hot features the same 'retro-swank' 1950s style c the restaurant. The 18 suites (some with wate views) have handcrafted furnishings an designer bathrobes, linens, glassware an excellent sound systems. Of course, as in th dining room downstairs, all this comes at price. $$$

Right: doorman at the Four Seasons

Inn at the Market
86 Pine Street
Telephone: 206 443-3600
www.innatthemarket.com
Perfectly central, cunningly hidden, the Inn at the Market is one of the most romantic hotels around. Many rooms have views of Puget Sound, and are beautifully decorated. Intimate and informal. $$$

MarQueen Hotel
600 Queen Anne Avenue N
Tel: 206 282-7407; www.marqueen.com
In the Queen Anne neighborhood, a few minutes walk from the Seattle Center. Old-fashioned and slightly hidden, dating back to 1918. Rooms are sweet, as are the staff, with an atmosphere like a bed-and-breakfast inn. $$

Mayflower Park Hotel
05 Olive Way
Telephone: (800) 426-5100, 206 623-8701;
www.mayflowerpark.com
This older hotel has an eclectic mix of rooms, some small and dark, some large and luxurious, not always related to the price, so check details when booking. That said, the Mayflower has lots of charm, particularly in the downstairs bar. $$$

Moore Hotel
926 2nd Avenue
Telephone: (800) 421-5508, 206 448-4852;
www.moorehotel.com

This hotel seems spartan once past the marbled lobby, but the small rooms are clean and the Downtown location can't be beat. $$

Pacific Plaza Hotel
400 Spring Street
Telephone: (800) 426-1165, 206 623-3900;
www.pacificplazahotel.com
Great value-for-money hotel within walking distance of Downtown, Pike Place Market and Pioneer Square. All rooms have cable, in-room movies and voice mail, and there's a complimentary continental breakfast. The lobby offers a bit of privacy, useful for holding business meetings, and the staff are helpful. $$

Panama Hotel
605 Main Street
Telephone: 206 223-9242
www.panamahotelseattle.com
The only hotel in the International District, this European-style hotel has bathrooms down the hall, but a rich history. Built in 1910, the building long housed immigrants and fishermen. Rooms, remodeled in the 1980s, have hardwood floors, antique furnishings and down comforters. Note: rooms above the street can be noisy. Weekly rates available. $-$$

Quality Inn & Suites Downtown Seattle Center
225 Aurora Avenue N
Telephone: 206 728-7666, (800) 255-7932;
www.seattleinn.com

bove: Hotel Edgewater – the Beatles fished from the window while here

Small but clean rooms at this conveniently-located chain motel, which has both an indoor pool and a Jacuzzi. $–$$

The Roosevelt
1531 7th Avenue
Tel: 206 621-1200; www.roosevelthotel.com
This 1929 hotel has all the benefits, and detriments, of its age. Oodles of charisma, particularly in the small lobby with a grand piano, but the less-expensive rooms are tiny. Best for those who don't blink at prices. $$$

Salish Lodge & Spa
6501 Railroad Avenue SE
Snoqualmie
Telephone: (800) 272-5474, 425 888-2556;
www.salishhotel.com
Located right at the top of the Snoqualmie Falls, the Salish is the ultimate rural treat for those visitors who yearn for the mountains and woods. Whirlpool tubs, fireplaces and custom-built furniture. Full spa on-site to pamper you after those long walks in the forest. $$$

Sixth Avenue Inn
2000 6th Avenue
Telephone: 206 441-8300
www.sixthavenueinn.com
A motel that's right Downtown. Good value for clean and undistinguished rooms. $$

Sorrento Hotel
900 Madison Street
Telephone: (800) 426-1265, 206 622-6400;
www.hotelsorrento.com
Built in 1909 when First Hill was a luxurious neighborhood and not 'Pill Hill' (named for the huge medical complexes), the Sorrento is a hidden architectural gem. Small and qui-etly elegant, discreet with excellent service. Suites are especially luxurious, and the views from the west side are truly spectacular. $$$

University Inn
4140 Roosevelt Way NE
Telephone: (800) 733-3855, 206 632-5055;
www.universityinnseattle.com
This is an upgraded former motel. Few rooms have bathtubs, but there's a generous complimentary breakfast and the inn is popular with visitors heading for the nearby University of Washington. $$

University Tower Hotel
4507 Brooklyn Avenue NE
Telephone: (800) 899-0251, 206 634-2000;
www.universitytowerhotel.com
Squarely in the University District, a snazzy hotel with great views (all bedrooms are large corner rooms). Reasonably priced, given the quality and service. $$–$$$

W Hotel
1112 4th Avenue
Telephone: 206 264-6000, (877) W-HOTELS;
www.starwoodhotels.com/whotels
Ultra-wired, ultra-fancy, Bladerunner meets German expressionist, with rooms equipped with CD players, feather comforters, and lots of pure linen. Of course there's fast internet access; this is the place for business travelers addicted to style. $$$

Watertown
4242 Roosevelt Way NE
Telephone: (866) 944-4242, 206 826-4242
www.watertownseattle.com
The newness of this 'urban hotel' shows in its clean style, amenities such as free high-speed Internet access and weekday evening wine bar. Five blocks from the University of Washington Seattle campus, the Watertown is just a few blocks from the Burke-Gilman Trail (You can go for a run, or borrow a bike and take a ride.) The complimentary breakfast bar is extensive. $$$

The Westin
1900 5th Avenue
Telephone: 206 728-1000, (800) WESTIN;
www.westin.com/seattle
Large businessperson's hotel, with great access

Above: Salish Lodge at the top of Snoqualmie Falls is the ultimate rural retreat

to Downtown; the location is also useful for shopping. The Westin's round twin towers are a good way to navigate, as they dominate the skyline in the area. $$

Pensiones and B&Bs

Bacon Mansion
959 Broadway Avenue E
Telephone: (800) 240-1864, 206 329-1864;
www.baconmansion.com
This Capitol Hill mansion looks like it's from the English countryside, but it's really just a 10-minute walk away from the bustle of mid-Broadway. Amenities include fireplaces, four-poster beds and a lovely antique tub. The rambling dining room makes it ideal for groups or large parties. $$$

Capitol Hill Inn
1713 Belmont Avenue
Tel: 206 323-1955; www.capitolhillinn.com
A small B&B with six themed rooms conveniently located within walking distance of Broadway stores and restaurants. Three-day minimum stay during peak season. $$

Chambered Nautilus B&B
5005 22nd Avenue NE
Telephone: 206 522-2536
www.chamberednautilus.com
A little noisy from the street, but thoughtful touches make this a favorite bed-and-breakfast place. $$

Pensione Nichols
1923 1st Avenue
Telephone: 206 441-7125, (800) 440-7125
Small B&B with an excellent location, right near Pike Place Market. Not much view (in fact, some rooms have just skylights), but the downstairs lounge makes up for it, with an expansive view over Puget Sound. $$

Shafer-Baillie Mansion
907 14th Avenue E
Telephone: 206 322-4654
www.shaferbaillie.tripod.com
Near Capitol Hill's Volunteer Park, a large converted mansion, built in 1914, with 11 rooms and suites and corridors that'll make you feel like you're in an English murder mystery. $$-$$$

Inexpensive Alternatives

College Inn Guest House
4000 University Way NE
Tel: 206 633-4441; www.collegeseattle.com
A 1909 building, with bathrooms at the end of each hall. Each room is spartan but clean. Located in the busy University District. $

Gaslight Inn
1727 15th Avenue
Tel: 206 325-3654; www.gaslight-inn.com
This Victorian house has a number of individual rooms, and is located in a quiet Capitol Hill neighborhood. Fun hosts, too. $$

Green Tortoise Backpackers Hostel
1525 2nd Avenue
Tel: 206 340-1222; www.greentortoise.net
Dorm-style rooms range from semi-public to semi-private. Located Downtown. $

Hostelling International Seattle
84 Union Street
Tel:206 622-5443; www.hiseattle.org
Male and female dorms and a communal kitchen. One block from Pike Place Market. Rooms close 11am to 4pm. $$

Vincent's Guest House
527 Malden Avenue E
Telephone: 206 323-7849
A youth hostel, but one with fewer rules. Some private rooms available. $$

Right: backpackers on a budget have several choices of where to stay

USEFUL INFORMATION

The **Seattle Visitor Information Center** (tel: 206 461-5840) is at the Washington State Convention & Trade Center, 800 Convention Place, Galleria Level, in downtown Seattle at the corner of 8th and Pike.

Disabled

Seattle can't always overcome geography. All city Metro buses are equipped with wheelchair lifts, but the steep hills of Downtown can pose problems. The Guided Tour (tel: 215 782-1370) offers good tours for people with disabilities. Alternatively, Wheelchair Getaways (tel: 888 376-1500 or 800 642-2042; www.wheelchair-getaways.com) rents vans with lifts for wheelchairs.

Health

The Emergency Services Number is **911**. Seattle has one of the world's most effective emergency response systems, and some of its hospitals, notably **Harborview**, have excellent trauma centers. In an emergency, you're in a great place, so don't worry and stay calm. Foreign citizens are advised to take out medical insurance as medicines and treatment are expensive.

Internet

Two good websites for local infor-
mation are Seattle-King County Convention and Visitor's Bureau, www.seeseattle.org, and the Washington State Tourism Office, www.experiencewashington.com. Internet cafés are few and far between, mainly clustered around Capitol Hill. Good coffee Aurafice (tel: 206 860-9977, 616 E Pine), Online Coffee Company (tel: 328-3731/381-1911, 1720 E Olive Way and 1111 1st Avenue). The area's 20-plus FedEx Kinko's locations have workstations onsite.

Mail

The midtown post office is located at 301 Union Street, tel: 206 748-5417; hours: 7:30am–5:30pm Monday–Friday. Travelers uncertain of their address can have mail sent care of General Delivery at the main post office. Stamps can be purchased in hotels, stores, airports and stations.

Sports

Seattle has a fine baseball team, the Mariners; a good football team, the Seahawks; and a basketball team, the Sonics. Even more fervently followed (although in smaller numbers) are the University of Washington Huskies and the professional women's basketball team, the Storm, which won the WNBA championship in 2004. Locals enjoy a range of sports including swimming, rowing, soccer, rock climbing and winter sports like snowboarding and skiing or ice-skating.

Telephone

The greater Seattle area has a single phone prefix, **206**, which you don't have to dial within the city. Many numbers on the Eastside have a prefix of **425**.

FURTHER READING

Insight Guide: Seattle
Apa Publications, Third edition, 2005
Essays on culture, history, geography, flora and fauna, plus information on nearby towns and cities. Full-color photographs and maps.
Insight Guide: Pacific Northwest
Apa Publications, Fourth edition, 2006
Local writers and photographers provide a comprehensive overview of the region, its cities, its people and its culture.

Above Left: the city has a very good emergency response system
Left: Seattleites are spoiled for sports choices. **Right:** clowning around

ACKNOWLEDGEMENTS

Photography	**Jerry Dennis** *and*
14B	**Bodo Bondzio**
16	**Getty Images**
12T	**Bruce Bernstein Collection/Courtesy Princeton University Library**
14T, 15	**Historical Society of Seattle and King County/Museum of History and Industry**
11	**Peter Newark's American Pictures**
16	**Courtesy of Text 100**
12B	**Courtesy of Underground Tours**
13	**R.F. Zallinger/Museum of Histroy and Industry**
Front cover	**Jerry Dennis**
Back cover	**Jerry Dennis**
Cartography	**Berndtson & Berndtson**
	James Macdonald

INDEX